*Heir to a culture that spans 60,000 years, an Aboriginal youth wears
a mask of mud while swimming in a Cape York water hole.*

Aust
Journey Through

Traces of a long-forgotten track dissolve in the haunting sands of Western Australia's Pinnacles Desert.

ralia

a Timeless Land

By Roff Smith

Photographs by Sam Abell

NATIONAL GEOGRAPHIC

WASHINGTON, D.C.

Contents

Cattle rancher Janice Bell and her children, like hundreds of other station folk, come in from the bush to take part in a Kimberley Championship Rodeo in the Western Australia town of Derby. With 28,000 inhabitants living in an area nearly twice as large as Britain, the Kimberley region of northwestern Australia is a surprisingly close-knit frontier. Events like the annual rodeo take on a family reunion quality.

Introduction

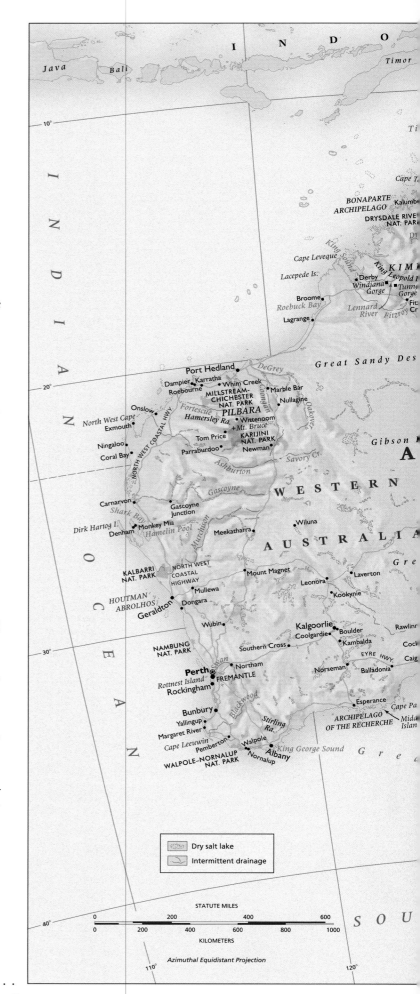

An island continent in a remote corner of the globe, Australia has tugged at the rest of the world's imagination since ancient Greek philosophers and geographers such as Aristotle and Pythagoras first postulated the existence of a Great Southern Land more than 2,000 years ago. They believed such a landmass must exist in order to keep the Earth in balance. Over the centuries lively medieval imaginations colored in this phantom continent with fabulous creatures and kingdoms. In 1606 Portuguese explorer Pedro Fernández de Quirós searched for it with the fervor of a Crusader, believing *Terra Australis Incognita* would prove to be a spiritual paradise. Different generations have different grails. To me, growing up in the snows of New England in the 1960s and '70s, Australia was a hazy collage of sunny images: The Sydney Opera House, Uluru, Bondi Beach, cricket matches, perpetual summers, and Land Rovers lurching down dusty red tracks. On my first trip to Australia, in 1982, I stepped off the plane marveling that autumn could be in March.

To the first European explorers the reality of Australia must have seemed as bizarre as fable. This was truly the land of upside down: Here the seasons were reversed, the swans were black, and strange trees lost their bark instead of their leaves. Marvels such as kangaroos, koalas, and platypuses lived in its fragrant bush, and the trees were so filled with raucous, brightly colored birds that early Spanish charts referred to the continent as *Terra Psittacorum*—land of parrots. When he wrote *Gulliver's Travels* in 1726, English author Jonathan Swift placed his fantasy country of Lilliput only a couple of days' journey, by canoe, from New Holland, as Australia was then known.

Forty-four years later, when James Cook's expedition sailed along Australia's luxuriant eastern shores, the profusion of strange plants and flowers they encountered in one inlet so excited the party's naturalists, Joseph Banks and Daniel Solander, that Cook named the place

Botany Bay. Later, when Cook's ship, the *Endeavour*, holed itself on the Great Barrier Reef along the coast of what is today far northern Queensland, the delighted Banks and Solander spent their enforced seven-week layover adding 180-odd new species of flora and fauna to their records.

Of course, Australia had quickened the imaginations of people eons before European explorers "discovered" the continent. Sixty thousand years ago an ancient Aboriginal people had come to these shores in what may well have been humanity's earliest major seafaring migration. Long before the Europeans' arrival they had mapped the land's great features, named its plants and birds and animals, recorded its history, come to understand its rhythms and seasons and complexities, and established their own unique metaphysical relationship with its warm, red earth. For thousands of generations they had passed on this knowledge, as well as their ethic of life, in a cycle of songs and dances, and had left rich legacies of rock art and engravings. Estimates vary. From 200,000 to 750,000 Aborigines were prospering in Australia at the time the 11 ships of the First Fleet sailed into Sydney Harbour in January 1788 to set up Britain's far-flung penal colony and political toehold in the South Pacific.

That landing brought irreparable changes to the Aborigines. Theirs was an ancient culture that treasured knowledge and skill above material possessions, but by the end of the 18th century they found themselves in conflict with a mighty European empire on the brink of the industrial revolution. Restless for land and fortune, gold and beef, wool for the textile mills, and coal to fire factory furnaces, the British shunted aside the original inhabitants and quickly took possession of the land. To the newcomers Australia was a primitive frontier, a raw-boned continent to be tamed and brought to profitable service as resolutely British colonies.

On January 1, 1901, six Australian colonies united to form a new nation. Its constitution spelled out just what kind of nation it would be: White, xenophobic, Anglo-Saxon, and vigorously loyal to England, whose monarch would remain its head of state. One of the new federal government's first acts as a nation was to proclaim the infamous White Australia immigration policy, which shut the door on most of the world's peoples. The Aborigines, who had been living on the land for thousands of generations, were almost completely ignored: They couldn't vote or run for office, and they were not even granted citizenship until 1967.

For much of the 20th century Australia was a plummy colonial anachronism—thriving in its sunny isolation at the bottom of the world. But even as its Anglophile Prime Minister Robert Menzies was proudly proclaiming himself British to his bootstraps in the 50s and 60s, big changes were afoot that would change the face of Australia forever. The booming years after World War II and through the 60s and 70s brought tens of thousands of immigrants from Italy, Greece, Malta, Turkey, Lebanon, Poland, Yugoslavia, West Germany, and Romania. The 1980s and '90s saw large influxes of Asians as Australia embraced multiculturalism with the zeal of the freshly converted.

Australia has always been a land of promise. Even for the miserable convicts, who were brought to the colony in chains and filth, there were potential opportunities here they could never have had back in the London slums. They were on the ground floor of the making of a new nation. Many finished their sentences and went on to own prosperous shops or gentlemanly farms. Some went into politics. And a spectacular few, like Samuel Terry, went on to acquire huge fortunes. Terry was an illiterate stonemason's laborer who had been banished to Australia in 1800 for stealing 400 pairs of stockings. The young colony needed strong backs and good builders. After serving his term, the astute convict promptly started his own building firm. Then, as the city prospered around him, he branched into real estate. By 1820 he was one of the wealthiest men in New South Wales, where he was known as the "Botany Bay Rothschild." He enjoyed an income of more than £10,000 pounds a year, and when he died in 1838 he left an estate worth £250,000 pounds—almost unimaginable wealth in those days.

But Australia offers something more than the potential for sunny prosperity. Over the past 20 years in particular it has matured into one of the world's most cosmopolitan, confident, and tolerant societies. People from more than 200 nationalities now call Australia home, melting together with an unbuttoned easiness that would be impossible almost anywhere else. It is a nation of nearly 19 million people, the vast majority of whom live in cities and suburbs within a half hour's drive of a beach.

Today, almost a century after proclaiming its nationhood, a relaxed and multicultural Australia is undergoing a period of quiet, mature reflection. No longer England's bucolic country cousins, distracted by historic ties to a distant and musty Europe no more, Australians increasingly look to a vibrant Asia for their future. And as Australians become more comfortable with their own uniqueness and position on the Pacific Rim, they are questioning some of the old institutions they grew up with—the English monarchy and the Union Jack on their flag. A majority of Australians now favor the idea of becoming a republic, with a new constitution and an elected president rather than the reigning British monarch as head of state.

With growing maturity and self-confidence, Australians have also taken a collective deep breath and begun to confront some of the ugly truths about their past. And they are trying to do something about that history, however painful facing it might be. In 1992 the Australian High Court ruled that the continent had not been *terra nullius*—no man's land—when Captain Cook claimed Australia on behalf of the Crown in 1770: The Aborigines had held a valid native title to the land. Subsequent rulings affirming that Aborigines are entitled to claim vacant crown land have prompted a rash of land claims around Australia, as well as howls of protest from the nation's mining and pastoral interests. Whatever the outcome of the myriad legal tangles, it is obvious that it will never again be possible to ignore the wishes of the first Australians.

For all its worldly flair, international cities, and vibrant multiculturalism, it is Australia's physical uniqueness that most captures the world's imagination and its photographic lenses. This is an entire continent—almost three million square miles—that went walkabout around 65 million years ago, preserving in its splendid isolation entire branches of the evolutionary tree that vanished

almost everywhere else: Marsupials, monotremes (egg-laying mammals) such as the platypus and the echidna, and living fossils such as the Jurassic period Wollemi pine that was found growing in a wild gorge little more than a hundred miles from downtown Sydney. The jewel-like Great Barrier Reef, the haunting monolith of Uluru, and the miracle of Kakadu National Park's wetlands are part of humanity's heritage.

Initiation rites in northern Australia's Arnhem Land tested the strength and will of young Aboriginal males. In the late 1920s candidates for manhood underwent a two-week-long series of trials. The third test demanded that they bake in the sun for a full day without food or water.

A trip to Australia remains one of the world's ultimate journeys. For many travelers it is an epoch-marking event in their lives, even if it goes unremarked at the time. I never came to this country expecting to be an immigrant, and although by now I've lived here almost all my adult life, until recently I still thought of myself as an American. So it came as a surprise to me several months ago when, after returning from a few months in the U.S., I gazed eagerly down at the barren South Australian landscape and the sight of Adelaide approaching in the distance and realized that the journey was taking me home.

Swollen by months of monsoon rain, the serpentine rivers of Australia's north turn dusty savanna into a vast wetland.

Fresh rains and rows of lavender soften the hills of Tasmania, a counterpoint to mainland Australia's arid outback.

As dusk slips over the Kimberley, the monstrous eye of a saltwater crocodile gleams in marshes near the port of Wyndham.

Catch in hand, an Aboriginal fisherman stalks rain-lashed shallows of the Gulf of Carpentaria in the Northern Territory.

Moonshine casts a spell over Western Australia's ancient Bungle Bungle Range.

Schools of wrasse and damselfish swirl among corals at the foot of Lord Howe Island, in the South Pacific Ocean.

Scourge of the outback—fire. A bolt of lightning can transform tinder-dry scrub into shooting flames and glowing embers.

Rock sentinels known as the Twelve Apostles—remnants of eroded cliffs—guard Victoria's storm-tossed Shipwreck Coast.

As day breaks at a station near Halls Creek, in the Kimberley, a jackaroo and his horses savor the predawn coolness.

Half-wild cattle forage hardscrabble earth dotted with termite mounds in Western Australia's rugged Kimberley.

CHAPTER ONE

The Far North

It was mid-September, near the end of the long dry season, and I was bouncing down a rough bush track toward the Gilbert and Staaten Rivers, extremely remote stretches of water that empty into far northern Queensland's Gulf of Carpentaria. I was traveling with local police constable Mick Jones; we were going fishing for barramundi. Northern Australia's finest, sweetest-eating game fish, barramundi lurk in the brackish mangroves and estuaries here—along with some of the world's largest and most dangerous saltwater crocodiles. It was the first time I had ever seen this part of Australia.

As I stared out the Land Cruiser window at miles of harsh scrub and endless savanna, I thought that even in a lifetime crowded with travel I had never seen any place more bleak and hostile. It had been seven months since the last rains fell. The ground was parched. Choking clouds of "bull dust," dust almost as fine as talc, drifted up from our footsteps and into our nostrils every time we stepped out to open gates along the track. Even with my lips clenched tight, I could taste it. The temperature was 110 degrees, the humidity was starting to build ahead of the coming monsoon, and the silvery leaves of the scrub hung limp in the torpid air. Insects whirred in the brittle grass. Farther out, the heat-warped horizon shimmered and wavered so much that it was impossible to tell where reality left off and mirage began. In another couple of months, when the monsoon hit, this would all be miles of marsh, mud, and riotous grass, and spectacular electrical storms would dance across purplish skies.

But now it was still and hazy and bright. Mick pulled over and stared out at one particularly desolate outlook.

After a few minutes of appreciative silence he slowly shook his head. "Beautiful, isn't it? I go away for a while but when I come back and see that, I know that I'm coming home." I smiled at him, wondering if he was joking. But, as I roamed Australia's far north over the next few months, I, too, began to appreciate its stark primal beauty: Its blood red sunsets, primeval mangrove swamps, ancient weathered gorges, the dangerous saltwater crocodiles that lurk in its brackish waters, and the eerie silhouettes of boab trees.

Australia's far north, also known as the Never Never in local parlance, is truly one of the planet's last great frontiers, stretching more than 3,000 miles from Queensland's Cape York Peninsula, through the Northern Territory's Arnhem Land, to the forbidding and little-known coasts of Western Australia's harsh Kimberley Plateau. It is a harsh and violent landscape, lashed by monsoons and tropical cyclones, swept by wild fires and floods of Biblical proportions, and roasted by summer temperatures that can soar to 120 degrees.

Few places on Earth are more treacherous. During the wet season a parched trickle like the Fitzroy River, in Western Australia, can turn almost overnight into a raging torrent 15 miles wide that washes away anything in its path. Old-time bushmen used to say that it was possible to die of thirst or drown in the same place, depending on what time of year a traveler was unlucky enough to be there. Other dangers await the unwary: Sharks and giant saltwater crocodiles and, in the hot summer months, the blood-warm seas can be awash with poisonous jellyfish. The tides up here are huge, fast, and powerful, and can rise nearly 40 feet in some places along the Kimberley coast. And everywhere in the dusty hinterland is a vast, almost conspiratorial silence reminiscent of the thousands of unexpected dangers or happenings that can make a luckless traveler disappear forever. As I bounced across the dusty gulf savanna in Mick's battered Land Cruiser that hot September afternoon, I couldn't help but notice how the hundreds of termite mounds dotting the landscape looked like so many abandoned gravestones in the crackly grass.

Wild and unspoiled as it is, Australia's far north has been the continent's gateway to the world for thousands of years. It has the longest and most cosmopolitan human history of any place on the continent, dating back more than 60,000 years to the arrival of the first Aborigines. Macassar fishermen started probing these ragged coasts 800 years ago. Dutch, French, Portuguese, Spanish, and English explorers followed them beginning in 1606. Chinese prospectors flocked to the goldfields in the Cape York Peninsula, the Kimberley, and the Northern Territory in the 1870s. The pearling industry, in remote locales like Broome and Thursday Island, brought hundreds of Japanese pearl divers, Malay and Filipino seamen, Indian and Arab jewelers, and polyglot adventurers and drifters from every steamy port in Asia and around the world. In 1872 an undersea telegraph cable linking Australia with the rest of the world was dragged ashore at Darwin. In the 1930s Karumba, on the Gulf of Carpentaria, was a staging post for Qantas flying boat service from Australia to the United Kingdom.

For a time the far north was Australia's front line during World War II, and silent clearings dotting the scrub south of Darwin are all that remain of once-vital British and American air bases. In the 1970s and 1980s desperate refugees from Vietnam staggered ashore here after surviving weeks at sea in flimsy boats, risking pirates, sharks, and storms. Even today, refugees from all parts of Asia occasionally float up to these wild coasts, gambling everything to reach the promise of Australia.

In a land whose history is salted with tales of epic sea voyages and daring adventures, it is a pity that so little is known about the grandest and boldest venture of all. Sometime around 60,000 years ago, or possibly even earlier, a fragile boat ground to a halt on a wild and far-flung beach on what was then the northern frontier of Aus-

tralia, and a seafarer splashed ashore. This was the first time a human being set foot on an entirely new continent. Until that moment—as far as we know—all of humanity had lived on the largely interconnected landmasses of Africa, Europe, and Asia. The Americas were still unknown and untouched. It would be another 45,000 years or so before tribes from Asia would cross the land bridge now covered by the Bering Strait and venture into North America. By then Australia's Aboriginal culture was already older than any continuous culture known today.

No one knows what brought the first Aborigines to Australia—war, famine, climate changes, or swashbuckling curiosity—or where they landed. Anthropologists speculate that they originally came from somewhere in Asia and trekked and island-hopped their way south over the course of many generations. The precise route that brought the first Aborigines to Australia remains a mystery, too. They might have sailed from Timor, an island in the Indonesian archipelago, to the Kimberley coast in northwest Australia. Or they might have come down through the Philippines, made landfall in New Guinea, and walked across the rest of the way, camping on the low, flat plains where the Gulf of Carpentaria is today.

The world was a very different place then, much cooler, and locked in the grip of an ice age that blanketed the higher latitudes with sheets of ice as much as a mile thick. So much of the planet's water was locked away in glaciers that sea levels were more than 400 feet lower than they are today. In those days islands such as Java and Bali were joined to the Asian mainland instead of being separated by shallow seas. There was no Torres Strait between Australia and New Guinea, and Australia's coastline stretched almost to the edge of the continental shelf. In Ice Age days it was no more than perhaps 45 miles from Timor to what was then the northern coast of Australia.

What is intriguing about these early voyages is that even a 45-mile journey would have taken these ancient seafarers well out of the sight and safety of land—a remarkable act of faith, considering they would have had no idea what lay over the horizon. What would have made them do it? Did they have myths of lands beyond the sea? Were their frail crafts blown there by storms? No one knows. But an ancient campsite in a remote corner of Kakadu National Park in the Northern Territory's Arnhem Land dates back an estimated 55,000 to 60,000 years, showing that Aborigines had certainly arrived by then.

Whatever their reasons for leaving their old homes in Asia, the first Australians were quick to seize upon the promise of the new, spreading out across the continent in every direction and making it their own. Archaeologists have found campsites in the Nepean Valley, near Sydney, that date back 45,000 years. Another site, near Melbourne's Tullamarine Airport, is more than 40,000 years old. In those Ice Age days it was possible to walk to Tasmania without getting your feet wet. Skeletal remains found in a cave near Hobart go back 35,000 years.

Australia was a gentler place then, cooler and greener, dotted with inland lakes and carpeted with rich grasslands. Game was plentiful and included fabulous animals and birds that have long since become extinct: kangaroos that stood ten feet high and wombat-like creatures larger than a rhinoceros. Thylacines, marsupial "tigers," roamed the continent.

There were changes in the wind, though—literally. Sometime about 18,000 years ago the Earth began to grow warmer. In Europe and North America the ice sheets began to melt, and as they did the sea level began an inexorable rise, creeping higher on the beaches and slowly submerging the coastal lowlands. To individual Aborigines living on Australia's fertile shores, the changes would have been almost imperceptible: perhaps a grandfather's memories of childhood days when the beach was farther away from camp. Over many generations, however, the changes were profound. By 8,000 years ago a narrow but ever widening strait had begun to divide Australia from New Guinea; the broad shallow plain where hundreds of generations of Aborigines had camped, hunted, and danced was well on its way to becoming today's Gulf of Carpentaria. Parts of Arnhem Land, Queensland's Cape York Peninsula, and Western Australia's Kimberley region—all once more than 150 miles from the sea—were within

earshot of rhythmic rollers that washed against the sands. And as the coastline shifted inland, mangrove swamps grew up and replaced savanna, while the warmer, drier climate transformed the interior of the continent into a vast swath of arid scrub.

Aborigines have primarily an oral culture, handing down their ancient traditions and Dreamtime stories from generation to generation in a complex cycle of songs and dances. But they left behind a priceless illuminated history painted in vibrant reds, purples, and ochers in rock-shelter galleries scattered across Arnhem Land, the Kimberley, and Cape York Peninsula. Together they offer a unique illustration of the landscapes, flora, fauna, and social changes in tropical northern Australia over the past 12,000 years or so.

The earliest paintings are of animals. The first depictions of humans, done in what archaeologists call the Dynamic style of art, illustrate a life of plenty: Finely sketched biceps of hunters and dancers ripple with athleticism. Elaborate feather headdresses are worn. Primitive kangaroos and thylacines appear. Landscapes were open savanna, where boomerangs were the weapons of choice. As the centuries passed and sea levels rose, the paintings began to include trees, water lilies, yams, and fish. Boomerangs became obsolete as savanna gave way to forest and mangrove. Hunters used spears instead. The Rainbow Serpent—a deity associated with creation—as well as floods and rain appear in the art.

The monsoon climate represented in the paintings apparently heralded trouble. A rock shelter in a remote gorge in Kakadu contains what some art historians believe to be the earliest known depictions of human beings in battle. One spectacular mural, 4,000 to 6,000 years old, shows 111 stick figures charging each other, hurling spears. Eight of the figures are falling, pierced by spears and spurting blood. Archaeologists interpret these conflicts as the result of global warming, when rising seas forced coastal people off their ancestral lands and onto the higher ground of their neighbors. It was around this time, about 6,500 years ago, that the seas stopped rising.

By then, Australia's northern coastline looked much the way it does today. Rising seas had flooded the lowlands in Southeast Asia, creating the Indonesian archipelago. Timor, a likely jumping-off place for ancient mariners, was now more than 200 miles from the nearest Australian landfall—a much more formidable voyage than the earliest migrants had faced. Even so, a final migration apparently took place about 5,000 years ago, the latecomers bringing with them a half-wild Asian camp dog that was to become Australia's dingo. After that, the remote island continent was largely cut off from the rest of the world, and dozed for centuries.

The first Europeans known to have visited Australia landed in 1606 on the Cape York Peninsula, near where the town of Weipa is today. Dutch navigator Captain Willem Jansz, commander of the *Duyfken—Dove*—had been sent by the directors of the Dutch East India Company to see what sort of spices, gold, and rare woods might be found in the Great Southern Land. He was unimpressed, reportedly describing it as a "waste land.... inhabited in some places by wild, cruel, black men and barbarians who killed some of our sailors."

A second Dutch expedition into these waters, in 1623, also failed to find any promise in the crocodile-infested mangroves and vast stretches of flat, dusty scrub along this wild coast. "It is very dry and barren for, during all the time we have searched and examined this part of the coast to our best ability," wrote Capt. Jan Carstensz, who led the 1623 expedition, "we have not seen one fruit-bearing tree, nor anything that man could make use of: there are no mountains or even hills, so that it may be safely concluded that the land contains no metals, nor yields any precious woods, such as sandalwood, aloes or columba. In our judgment this is the most barren region that could be found anywhere on earth."

Whatever these Dutchmen thought of the scenery, they were certainly wrong about the Cape York Peninsula's lack of minerals. Ironically they had landed almost on top of the world's largest deposit of bauxite—the ore used to make aluminum. Since the mid-1960s the far-

flung outpost of Weipa (population 2,200) has supported the giant Comalco bauxite mine, worth millions to the Australian economy.

If the early Dutch visitors were too dismissive, 19th-century British empire-builders held grandiose (and equally inaccurate) ambitions for this remote peninsula. Jutting into Torres Strait, only 150 miles from New Guinea and on what was then a major East Indies shipping route, the tip of Cape York seemed the ideal place to build a trading city—another Singapore. In 1863 the Queensland government sent John Jardine, a former police magistrate from Rockhampton, to the tip of the peninsula—at 10 degrees 41 minutes 21 seconds south latitude, the northernmost point in Australia—to establish the new city. It was called Somerset, after the Duke of Somerset, then Lord of the Admiralty.

To keep the outpost supplied, the Queensland government commissioned Jardine's two tough young sons, Frank and Alexander, to drive a mob of cattle from Rockhampton north through more than a thousand miles of uncharted bush, swamp, and jungle to Somerset. It was a formidable undertaking. The only previous attempt to travel the length of Cape York had been a disastrous expedition led by Edmund Kennedy in 1848. Of 13 men who set out, just three survived; only the group's Aboriginal guide had actually reached the tip. Kennedy had been killed by hostile Aborigines a few miles short of his goal.

The Jardine brothers set out in May 1864 with 8 men, 42 horses, 250 head of cattle, and a lot of ambition. Over the next few months they hacked their way north through the scrub. They lost most of their horses and cattle, but every man survived to reach Somerset the following March. Their remarkable achievement, however, was marred by the ferocity with which they treated Aborigines along the way. Adopting a shoot-first-and-don't-bother-asking-afterward policy, the gung ho party bulled their way up the peninsula leaving a trail of corpses. Their ruthlessness culminated in a bloody battle on the Mitchell River in which 30—and possibly more—Aborigines were gunned down.

Somerset, the would-be Singapore that was the focus of so much effort and bloodshed, never grew beyond 200 inhabitants. Termites, fevers, cyclones, and hostile Aborigines took their toll, and in 1877 the

Queensland government had the inhabitants evacuated to nearby Thursday Island, where a pearling industry was just getting started. Frank Jardine, however, remained in the area, running a string of cattle stations in northern Cape York. Much admired by colonial authorities, he was hated and feared by the Aborigines. Local legend has it that after he died of leprosy in 1919, the Aborigines secretly reburied him, head pointed downward, to make certain that his murderous spirit could never return.

Today, the Cape York Peninsula remains one of Australia's wildest and least inhabited frontiers. A gold rush in the southern part of the peninsula during the 1870s lured thousands of fortune hunters to this wilderness. They left, however, almost as quickly when the pay dirt grew scarce, and once rollicking settlements, such as Maytown and Laura, are virtually silent now. Most of the few people up here live in isolated Aboriginal communities and cattle stations. Roads are few and rough, and most residents receive mail once a week from a single-engine Cessna that flies out of Cairns. Only the mail run through South Australia's remote deserts is longer.

Traveling overland to the Tip, as the peninsula is known, is one of Australia's great four-wheel-drive adventures. The route stretches across 500 miles of wild, axle-breaking bush track from Cooktown to Bamaga, an isolated community perched just inland of the Torres Strait about a hundred miles from New Guinea. Challenging at any time of year, the roads become impassable during the wet season, and the handful of isolated towns and roadhouses along the way are cut off from the rest of the world. Even in the dry season, a number of challenging river crossings (beware of crocodiles!) have to be made. The swamps, rain forests, and marshes cursed by the likes of Kennedy and the Jardines more than a century ago are today cherished national parks.

Lakefield National Park, with its vast tidal mudflats, lagoons, and primeval marshes, is particularly noted for its conservation of saltwater crocodiles. About 120 miles farther north the track winds through the rain forests of the southern segment of Mungkan Kandju National Park,

a million acres of preserved wilderness where the Coen and Archer Rivers flow down from the jungle-clad McIlwrath Range. Near the northern end of the peninsula lies the magnificent Jardine River National Park, with its lush rain forests, the stately Jardine River and a large population of crocodiles. Fording the wide and sandy Jardine River is the last major barrier for travelers before reaching Bamaga—and ultimately the Tip. The ruins of Somerset and the lonely graves of Frank Jardine and his family lie just a few miles away. These relics of conquest and ruthless colonial ambition are today an easy day trip for visitors to the elegant Pajinka Lodge, a popular wilderness resort owned and operated by the local Injinoo Aborigines.

West along the rim of the Gulf of Carpentaria lies wide, hot gulf savanna country that has hardly changed since 1861, when explorers Robert O'Hara Burke and William John Wills struggled through it during the Wet on an epic south-to-north crossing of the continent. The harshness of the scenery came as a surprise to me when I first traveled through here. Since the south end of the Gulf of Carpentaria lies at roughly the same latitude as Cairns, I had expected this tropical coast to be green and lush with rain forests. Instead it was burned brown and shimmering with heat, except for mangrove swamps along the immediate coast.

The settlements out here have a tough, frontier atmosphere that isn't to everybody's taste. A remote refueling stop for Qantas flying boats in the 1930s, the outpost of Karumba today is a fishing port with a reputation for roughness and a pub known as the Animal Bar.

I went in for a drink one afternoon when the fleet was in and found myself talking with about six-foot-four inches of hardened, heavily-tattooed ex-con, one of about a dozen mallet-fisted drinkers loitering around the bar. Fortunately we got along. On a return visit the next afternoon I found myself confronted at the pool table by a weaselly man who looked like his knife work would be efficient. My drinking buddy of the previous day drifted by and said hello. The other bloke went pale and remembered he had to be somewhere else.

Thirty miles east of Karumba is Normanton, another frontier town on the Norman River. The largest saltwater crocodile ever recorded—just over 28 feet long, with the build of a modest-size dinosaur—was reputedly shot on the banks of the Norman in 1957. There is no shortage of its snaggle-toothed relatives lurking in the river and mangrove swamps today.

A hundred and forty miles farther west on a rough and lonely gravel road is Burketown. One of outback Australia's most isolated communities, it is sometimes cut off from the rest of the world for weeks at a time when monsoon rains flood the low savanna. Burketown marks the western edge of the Gulf of Carpentaria's savanna grasslands and the beginning of the wetlands that stretch north and west towards the primeval wilderness of Arnhem Land and the frontier city of Darwin, capital of the Northern Territory.

Darwin surprises a lot of first time visitors, who typically step off the plane expecting to find themselves in a set for *Crocodile Dundee*. Instead, they discover a bright, modern cosmopolitan city of 80,000, with a spread of neat suburbs and shopping malls. At first glance only the tropical flowers in the gardens, the soporific heat, and the dazzling turquoise blue of the Timor Sea seem to give Darwin a sense of location; otherwise it could be a big Melbourne suburb. But look at a map. This toehold of suburbia is the only settlement of any size on Australia's entire 3,000-mile inhospitable northern coast, and it is the focus of activity for this region of the Northern Territory—an area known as the Top End. Less than an hour's drive south on Daly Street is desolate scrub; two hours east lie the primeval wetlands of Kakadu National Park—landscapes unchanged in thousands of years. Saltwater crocodiles still appear on occasion in the suburbs of Darwin, and in the summer its beaches are so full of deadly jellyfish that swimming is banned.

The reason the buildings and office blocksof this low-slung city appear so new is because they are: Darwin was nearly wiped off the map by Cyclone Tracy, which roared into the city on Christmas Day 1974 packing winds of up to 160 miles an hour. Most of the colonial buildings and wooden houses built, tropical style, on stilts are gone, replaced by (it is hoped) cyclone-proof architecture.

Darwin's history is a litany of tenacious rebuilding. It has been blown down by cyclones several times, bombed by the Japanese in World War II, and in its early days eaten by termites. A weather station in the city now tracks cyclones that might threaten it. Although Darwin is regarded as the last frontier, it was actually one of the first places settled by the British. After establishing convict colonies in Sydney, in 1788, and in Hobart, in 1804, the Colonial Office decided it would be prudent to plant the flag in the northern part of the continent to thwart French and Dutch ambitions in the area. Matthew Flinders, the English navigator who circumnavigated the continent in 1803, had repeatedly bumped into his French counterpart, Nicholas Baudin, on his travels. Baudin was also surveying the Great Southern Land. His charts were sprinkled with French names, Joseph Bonaparte Gulf, Cape Leveque, Cape Dussejour, and, most ominously in those days of empire, he referred to the continent as Terra Napoleon.

In 1818 the British established a settlement at Port Essington that was soon abandoned. In August 1824 Captain J. J. Gordon Bremer was dispatched from Sydney to set up a military outpost, Fort Dundas, on Melville Island. It was a miserable place. Tropical fevers, termites, the dreary monsoons, and hostility from the Tiwi Islanders, on whose land the colonists were trespassing, forced the British to abandon the outpost by 1829. Another attempt, Fort Wellington at nearby Raffles Bay, lasted only from 1827 to 1829.

Still fearing that the French would try to establish a colony here, the British reestablished the settlement at Port Essington in 1838. Sure enough, a few days after the Union Jack was run up the pole and the new outpost christened Victoria, after Britain's new queen, two French ships appeared on the horizon. They were the *Astrolabe* and the *Zelee*, under the command of Captain Dumont d'Urville, ostensibly on an exploratory expedition around Australia. Plagued by disease, termites, and the harsh tropical climate, Victoria fared no better than the other efforts. It was abandoned by 1849. Present-day Darwin dates from 1869. It was originally called Palmerston, but was known by sailors for the harbor on which it was sited: Port Darwin. It had been named after the celebrated naturalist who passed this way on the *Beagle* in 1839.

Soon the brawling seaport, which flourished on the back of a gold rush in the 1880s, became known around Southeast Asia as Port Darwin. It was officially renamed Darwin in 1911. The town might have taken its new name sooner, but until 1911 the administration of the Northern Territory was in the hands of prim and religious South Australians who had little regard for Charles Darwin and his evolutionary monkeys.

The town's residents had no such reservations. Certainly there was nothing particularly godly about early Darwin. Consider this description by poet and columnist Andrew Barton "Banjo" Paterson when he visited the Top End in 1898: "Palmerston on Port Darwin…is unique among Australian towns, inasmuch as it is filled with the boilings over of the great cauldron of Oriental humanity. Here comes the vagrant and shifting population of all the Eastern races…all sorts and conditions of men. Kipling tells what befell the man who 'tried to hustle the East,' but the man who tried to hustle Palmerston would get a knife in him quick and lively."

A century later Darwin is still a swirl of races and creeds, but the xenophobia and racism of Banjo Paterson's day has been replaced by a proud multiculturalism. Darwin is as much a gateway to Asia as it is a toehold on Australia's wild frontier. More than 60 nationalities can be found in this exotic city. Evenings I have spent strolling among the food stalls at Darwin's Mindil Beach markets felt as though I were in Asia rather than outback Australia. The warm tropical air is generally redolent with spices, scorched chilies, and hot cooking oil. Satay, *laksa*, and *nasi goring* are among the foods for sale. Families set up folding chairs and tables on the beach, and in a medley of Asian and European languages, chatter amongst themselves as they watch the sun sink into the Timor Sea.

Late in the spring, as thunderheads start to build ahead of the coming monsoon, the sunset markets close. The gregarious town becomes moody and introverted, battening down mental and physical hatches for the long, oppressive summer months of heat, humidity, torrential rains, and tropical cyclones. The Wet, as the monsoon season is known, can be as dreary and draining in its way as the long darkness of a Scandinavian winter. Life slows to a torpid, irascible crawl. Everything, it seems, is put on hold until after the Wet. Life in the far north is portioned into two main seasons—the Wet and the Dry. The dry season typically runs from May through October, the Australian winter, when the temperature drops into the low 80s and the skies are a taut blue for weeks at a time. Creeks dry up, savanna grasses wither, and water holes shrink to shimmering puddles of mud with cracks around the edges.

Then, through the spring months of October and November, the temperature and humidity start their inexorable rise. Over the Gulf of Carpentaria, spectacular tubular cloud formations called the "morning glory" appear at dawn. By the heat of the afternoon, all across the tropical north of the continent, towering cumulus clouds, built by thermals, are scudding across the horizon.

Hot nights pulse with distant flashes of lightning, promising but rarely delivering any stormy relief from the oppressive humidity. Occasionally, a stray bolt of lightning strikes the earth, sparking a wildfire in the tinder-dry brush that can blacken tens of thousands of acres and redden sunsets with its smoke. I have camped in the bush on such stifling nights, wondering whether the tickling I felt was ants or sweat (it was both) and watching an evil-looking fire ring a distant hillside. Locals call these relentlessly sweaty months the Build-up. A universal grumpiness seems to settle over the region. Mates snap at each other for no good reason, and police blotters fill up with cases of petty assaults and drunkenness of those who have "gone troppo." The rains usually start to fall late in December. Day after day of torrential monsoon, thunder, and purplish black skies grip the tropical northern towns with gloom. In Darwin the pace of life slows to a sullen crawl, and many of those who can afford to go elsewhere retreat to the sunny coolness of the south.

In the bush, however, the rains bring a celebration of life that would shame Hieronymus Bosch. Withered scrub is suddenly transformed into a fantasy of ferns, marsh, and riotous grasses that can grow more than 15 feet in a single month. Desert canyons sprout thundering cataracts and waterfalls. Flat, dusty plains become broad wetlands teeming with bird life. Nowhere is this miraculous transformation more spectacular than in Kakadu National Park, a World Heritage site about 80 air miles southeast of Darwin.

At nearly five million acres, Kakadu is Australia's largest national park and ranks with the Great Barrier Reef as one of the most popular. Kakadu encompasses almost the entire drainage basin of the South Alligator River and a little of every kind of habitat Australia's far north has to offer. It shelters a remarkable assemblage of flora and fauna that includes some 280 bird species, 128 species of reptiles, 64 native mammal species, 51 varieties of freshwater fish, 1,600 species of plants, and more than 4,500 species of insects.

Kakadu includes a portion of the 300 mile-long Arnem Land Escarpment and part of the Arnhem Land Plateau within its boundaries. The escarpment is a chain of sheer sandstone cliffs that rise hundreds of feet above the low, flat woodlands and form the edge of the Arnhem Land Plateau. When the monsoons arrive, typically dropping almost five feet of rain in a few torrential weeks, the waterlogged plains form vast freshwater wetlands, and the excess rainwater spills over the edge of the escarpment in a series of magnificent waterfalls. Two of the most spectacular—and frequently photographed—are Twin Falls and Jim Jim Falls. At Jim Jim the thundering water tumbles, including one sheer, heart-stopping pitch of 590 feet, more than 700 feet. Niagara Falls, by comparison, drops a paltry 167 feet.

One day, usually early in May, the rains cease; the sun breaks through the shredding clouds; and mists rise from the drenched earth. This is the start of the dry season. No more rains come. Day after day, week after week, there is nothing but faultless blue sky and dazzling sun. The waterfalls dry up; the water holes recede to little pools ringed by patches of shiny mud. By July the jungly undergrowth has withered and faded from lush arsenic green, through a suite of yellows, to brown, and finally black. Wildlife congregates around the shrinking water holes. Of these, one of the favorites among visitors to Kakadu, is Cooinda, an oasis of raucous flocks of birds, luxuriant water plants, and large crocodiles sunning themselves in the mud.

After six months of dry weather, the humidity starts to rise. Lightning dances once again on the horizon. The sun rises red from the smoke of distant bushfires. It is time for the cycle to begin anew.

Farther west, in the corner of the continent, lies an ancient, gnarled region known as the Kimberley: a place so vast and remote it is virtually a world unto itself. It is immense— about 139,000 square miles of dramatic mountain ranges, sweeping tidal flats, and a ragged, treacherous coast that has hardly changed since Dutch navigator Abel Tasman skirted it in 1644.

Despite its size—almost twice as large as Great Britain—there are only three towns of more than 2,000 people in all of the Kimberley: Derby, Kununurra, and the colorful old pearling port of Broome. The biggest of these towns, Broome, has about 9,000 inhabitants. The remainder of the Kimberley's population of 25,000 live in isolated cattle stations, mining camps, Aboriginal communities, and dusty towns scattered like a landlocked archipelago across this craggy, billion-year-old wilderness. The nearest big city, Perth, lies more than a thousand miles to the south, far beyond the implacable void of the Great Sandy Desert that makes up the Kimberley's southern flank. To the north lie the turquoise blue waters of the Timor Sea, over which Australia's first inhabitants came about 60,000 years ago. The original coastline they knew was long ago submerged by rising seas after the Ice Age, erasing forever their earliest settlements and sacred sites. But the secluded caves and rock shelters across the Kimberley hinterland are rich in vibrant rock art galleries and murals.

My first glimpse of the Kimberley came several years ago from the window of a chartered twin-engine turboprop. It was flying workers into the secluded Argyle Diamond Mine, which is nestled in the Ragged Ranges about a hundred miles south of Kununurra. It was a hot and humid morning early in March, near the end of the wet season. As we droned through the clear, blue Kimberley sky, the plane pitched and bounced in the thermals. Now the diamond miners drive to the Argyle for two-week shifts, but then this flight from Kununurra was a daily routine for them. They resolutely read their dog-eared novels, but I was glued to the spectacle spreading out beneath the little plane's wings. Recent rains had made the desert bloom. Luxuriant tropical grasses rioted where only a few weeks earlier there had been nothing but reddish blistered stone. Magnificent waterfalls tumbled over cliffs, and cataracts sparkled in far off gorges.

The sense of adventure and the romance was heightened by the knowledge that ahead, in the hazy distance, lay the world's largest diamond mine: A craggy, well-guarded hilltop where more than 38 million carats of raw diamonds are produced each year, more than one-third of the planet's entire output. Jewels from the Argyle come in a range of exotic colors: Champagne, cognac, green, blue, and, rarest of all, pinks that have fetched up to one million dollars a carat in the hushed showrooms of New York and Amsterdam. These are diamonds so remote, according to the company's marketing blurb, "that it took three billion years to find them."

Forty-five minutes after taking off from Kununurra, the little plane touched down at the mine's private airfield. The workers trundled off to their jobs, and I began a fascination with the Kimberley that has brought me back time and again.

The Kimberley contains some of Australia's most spectacular and least visited natural wonders: Roaring tidal waterfalls at Talbot Bay, fossilized remains of a huge Devonian Age coral reef, and the dramatic Wolfe Creek Meteorite Crater. Perhaps the most magnificent sight in the Kimberley is the haunting maze of tiger-striped sandstone domes known as the Bungle Bungles. Although sacred to local Aborigines for more than 20,000 years and known to a handful of Kimberley pastoralists for the past century, the ancient formations were virtually unknown to the outside world until the early 1980s. A filmmaker shooting a documentary about the splendor of the Kimberley captured some aerial footage of the Bungle Bungles glowing coppery bronze in the warmth of an afternoon. The stunning images immediately captured the public's imagination. Today, the timeless spectacle of the Bungle Bungles epitomizes the primeval power and

grandeur of the Kimberley. In 1987 they were included in Purnululu National Park. Like most places in the Kimberley, much of it must be explored by four-wheel drive or seen by air.

Because of its remoteness, the Kimberley was the last region of Australia to be explored by European settlers, and until relatively recently it was still a land only for outback-hardened prospectors, pioneers, and adventurers. Mail deliveries by packhorse, the sails of the pearling luggers setting out to sea, the much anticipated steamer that came up the coast from Fremantle every few weeks—images that seem to come straight from the pages of a Joseph Conrad novel—are within the memories of people still living. Telephone service and television did not arrive in the outlying stations and communities until the 1980s. The region's main highway, which skirts its southern edge, wasn't paved until 1986. The Kimberley's earliest European history—the explorers, gold rushes, epic cattle drives—is no further removed than the parents and grandparents of families such as the Emanuels, the McDonalds, and the Duracks.

The region was named the Kimberley by the West Australian government in 1880 to honor Britain's Secretary of State for the Colonies, the first Earl of Kimberley. Its hinterland was first crossed by explorer Alexander Forrest in 1879-1880. His glowing reports of good grazing country drew a rush of cattlemen in the 1880s, some of whom drove mobs of cattle across the stony heart of the continent to stake their claims.

One of the most dramatic cattle drives in history—and, at 3,500 miles, the world's longest—was made by the McDonald family, whose descendants still own the million-acre Fossil Downs cattle station in the heart of the Kimberley. Starting near Goulburn, New South Wales, with just over 700 head of cattle, the family headed northwest in March 1883, taking three years to cross the continent.

That same year the Durack family left their homes in the Cooper Creek region of southwest Queensland bound for the Kimberley. The story of their epic two-year cattle drive and early struggles to settle along the giant Ord River and near the Bungle Bungles is chronicled in Dame Mary Durack's outback classics *Kings in Grass Castles* and *Sons in the Saddle*.

A short-lived gold rush near Halls Creek in 1885 brought a rapid influx of 10,000 prospectors and fortune seekers to the Kimberley. Most were disappointed. Faced with the harsh conditions, tropical heat, and summer monsoons, they left as rapidly as they had come, but some stayed on.

In the 1860s the discovery of rich pearling grounds off the coast of Broome had lured adventurers from all around southeast Asia. The fledgling port was gazetted as a town in 1883. Ironically, the man for whom Broome was named, West Australia Governor Sir Frederick Napier Broome, was deeply offended that his name had been given to such a rough shantytown. He was sure the settlement wouldn't last more than a few years. Few Australians today remember who or what Sir Frederick was, but almost everybody aspires to visit the famed "port of pearls" that bears his name.

Broome, in the region's far southwest, is without doubt the prettiest town in the Kimberley. Its oasis-like setting, turquoise seas, and exotic Asian atmosphere reflect its colorful past as a pearling port. From the tourist point of view, Broome is the only town in the Kimberley to have a beach rather than looking out on miles of grim-looking tidal mudflats. And what a beach. Some two miles west of the town center are the vast white sands of Cable Beach, so named because this is where an undersea telegraph cable from Java was dragged ashore in 1889. Several hundred yards wide at low tide, and stretching for more than 15 miles, Cable is often rated one of the world's most beautiful and unspoiled beaches, and the low-key luxury resort built nearby in the 1980s is frequently ranked among Australia's best.

But it was pearls, not scenery, that gave Broome its start in the 1860s. By 1900 the rich seabeds of Roebuck Bay had made Broome the world's pearling capital. It boasted a polyglot population of more than 5,000 and a fleet of some 400 pearling luggers putting out to sea. The boisterous community was a bewildering swirl of races and cultures: Japanese, Malays, Filipinos, Chinese, Indonesians, Aborigines, Indians, Melanesians, Pacific Islanders, and an assortment of European adventurers, drifters, and rapscallions from all over the world. Pearling was a fast-money, dangerous occupation, as the crowded Japanese cemetery on the edge of town can attest. Many of the occupants were young men, killed by the bends, cyclones, or sharks.

The Great Depression and World War II—during which Broome was bombed by the Japanese—put Broome's pearling industry into a long decline. The introduction of plastic buttons during the war nearly killed it off, since there was no longer a market for the mother-of-pearl that had been the town's mainstay. A small but reliable demand for pearls kept the fading town alive until it was "discovered" in the 1980s. An Englishman, Lord McAlpine, became so enamored of Broome that he poured millions into the town and developed the prestigious Cable Beach Resort.

His lordship later fell onto financial hard times, but Broome's nascent tourist industry prospered on his investments and today is one of Australia's most cherished and romantic destinations. Visitors range from backpack travelers and drifters to well-heeled tourists who apparently can afford the five- and six-figure price tags on the fine pearl jewelry offered by the cluster of boutiques in town.

Yet for all Broome's big-money resort development, its streets shaded by mango and palm trees, the slow pace of life locals call "Broome time," and quaint institutions such as the Sun Picture Gardens exert a lazy, tropical charm. Billed as the world's oldest open-air movie theater, the Sun is little changed since it opened in 1916. Patrons sit in canvas sling chairs under a wooden shelter and watch an outdoor screen framed by palm fronds. I watched W. C. Fields and Mae West in *My Little Chickadee* there a few years ago, munching popcorn and watching fruit bats chase night insects across the screen.

A hundred miles farther north is Derby, a remote town of about 3,000 perched on the edge of a vast sprawl of mudflats in King Sound. Despite its lonely, almost apocalyptic setting, when the town was declared in 1883, Derby entertained lofty ambitions as a commercial center for the pastoralists of the West Kimberley. It was named for then Secretary of State for the Colonies, the 15th Earl of Derby. A jetty was built in 1885, and thousands of prospectors passed through here on their way to the Halls Creek goldfields about 300 miles inland.

Treacherous and powerful tidal currents at the entrance to the sound made Derby a difficult and dangerous port, and a phenomenal 36-foot tidal range in the harbor left ships sitting on the mud at low tide. Today cargoes are loaded onto shallow-draft barges and relayed to bulk carriers anchored in deep water well offshore, and Derby is better known as an airfreight and communications center for the West Kimberley.

Derby was the northern terminus for Australia's first airmail service, which began flying between Geraldton and the isolated Kimberley seaport in 1921. Later Derby became a base for the Royal Flying Doctor Service, and its hospital is the biggest and best equipped in the Kimberley. For many visitors, however, the town is best known as a terminus of the Gibb River Road, famed as one of the most dramatic four-wheel driving adventures in Australia. A dubious shortcut, about 150 miles shorter than the paved highway, the Gibb River Road stretches from Derby nearly 450 miles through the heart of the Kimberley to the old port of Wyndham.

The route crosses the dramatic King Leopold Range and skirts some of Australia's most remote national parks. The highway was begun in the 1960s to help isolated cattle stations bring their livestock to market. Locals still refer to it as the Beef Road, and travelers along it are warned to be careful of the huge triple-rigged road trains that rumble along in a shower of gravel and bull dust.

For tourists venturing along it in the dry season, the Gibb is the road back through time to a fossilized coral reef that once would probably have rivaled today's Great Barrier Reef. At Windjana Gorge, about 80 miles east of Derby, the Lennard River cuts a narrow three-mile path through this ancient limestone complex, lush with palms, rife with freshwater crocodiles, and noisy with a wide variety of birds.

In the 1890s this lost world was the hideout of Jandamarra, a famously elusive Aborigine guerrilla fighter who conducted a spirited campaign to stave off white occupation of the Kimberley. Known to the settlers as Pigeon, he tried to organize local Aboriginal groups to march on Derby and drive the whites out of the Kimberley. Jandamarra was eventually tracked down and killed

near Tunnel Creek Gorge in 1897, but Aboriginal resistance to the takeover of their lands continued long after his death. As late as the 1930s Aborigines occasionally speared unwary travelers in the Kimberley.

Not all Kimberley Aborigines were hostile to the pioneers, however. Many offered their remarkable bush skills to the newcomers, and although they had never raised cattle before, Aborigines quickly became known as some of the finest riders and wranglers on the range. Indeed, many early pioneers owed their success to the hard work of Aborigines.

About a third of the way along the Gibb River Road is a turn-off for an isolated mission at Kalumburu, on the ragged northern edge of the Kimberley coast. The mission is about 165 miles north along a rough bush track made impassable much of the year by heavy monsoon rains.

This wild, northern fringe of Australia contains some of the Kimberley's most magnificent scenery: Gorges thick with ancient fan palms and rare species of plants found nowhere else, giant cascades that form Mitchell Falls, and the hidden splendor of 4,000-square-mile Drysdale River National Park. This pristine wilderness is possibly Australia's most remote national park, an untouched wonderland of swamps, ranges, and pockets of rain forest that are accessible only by helicopter or by canoe down the wild Drysdale River. A scientific expedition to this hidden corner of the Kimberley in 1975 turned up dozens of new species of plants.

The Gibb River Road joins the main highway near Wyndham, an isolated cattle-shipping port of 700 at the mouth of the King River. "The thermometers, and the mosquitoes are three feet high," wrote travel writer Ernestine Hill when she passed through here in the 1930s. Nestled at the foot of Mount Bastion, Wyndham is the most hauntingly remote settlement I have ever seen. Forbidding hills behind the town seem to shoulder out the rest of the world. The view from Five Rivers Lookout, at the top of the mountain, however, is as breathtaking as it is timeless: A shimmering expanse of crocodile-infested tidal flats where five of the biggest rivers in the Kimberley—the Ord, Pentecost, Durack, Forrest, and King—sluggishly meet the Cambridge Gulf.

For most of the past century Wyndham's main industry was the meat works, where Kimberley cattle were slaughtered before export. Until it closed in 1985, this frontier abattoir offered the few sightseers that came up this way one of the Kimberley's most gruesome spectacles: The snouts of scores of giant saltwater crocodiles waiting expectantly in the marshes near the outflow of the blood drain. The closure of the meat works hit the town—and, presumably, its population of crocodiles—hard, but in the past few years its fortunes have picked up. Today Wyndham is an export center for the Kimberley's live-cattle trade with Asia and the Middle East. It is also a shipping port for the burgeoning sugar industry and market gardens in the giant Ord River Irrigation Scheme that is centered around the town of Kununurra, some 50 miles east. The site of the old meat works is now a successful crocodile farm.

Kununurra is by far the youngest town in the Kimberley, laid out in 1961 as part of an ambitious plan to create fertile farmland from remote tropical scrub. For the better part of a century the West Australian government had been trying to figure out what to do with its grand northwest frontier.

Despite its year-round warmth, sunshine, and vast tracts of rich clay soil, the Kimberley's savagely lopsided climate of torrential monsoon rains followed by months of earth-cracking drought had defeated every attempt to grow crops. During the wet season the Ord River is Australia's most powerful flow of water, roaring down the flanks of the Durack Range and uselessly dumping more than 13 million gallons of water each second into the Cambridge Gulf. Why not dam the Ord? If the water could be rationed throughout the year, it was reasoned, the river's broad floodplain could be turned into an irri-gated garden. Experimental farms during the 1930s and 1940s successfully grew cotton, sorghum, maize, rice, sugar, and linseed along the Ord.

In 1958 the Ord River project was born. Millions of dollars were poured into dams, irrigation systems, and the building of the township of Kununurra. A small diversionary dam got the project under way, and by 1966 there were 31 farms along the Ord River.

In 1972 the centerpiece of the project, the huge Ord River Dam, was completed, inundating an 18,000-year-old Aboriginal campsite as well as the pioneering Argyle Downs Station. In their place was the giant 380-square-mile Lake Argyle; a small inland sea that holds more than 18 times the volume of Sydney Harbour. An impressive feat of remote-area engineering, the Ord River project was also for many years Australia's most expensive white elephant. Nothing seemed to go right. Crop prices were unexpectedly low, and costs were unexpectedly high. Silt problems threatened to clog the dam. Caterpillars ate the cotton crops, while thousands of magpie geese flocked to the area to feast at the fledgling rice fields. Many farmers sold out and quit.

But those who managed to stay are today reaping the rewards. The Ord River's nearly 35,000 acres of irrigated farmland produce rich crops of peanuts, mangoes, melons, cucumbers, bananas, sunflowers, and sorghum. In 1996 Australia's first new sugar mill in almost 70 years was built near Kununurra to handle the Kimberley's burgeoning sugar industry. Kelly's Knob, a rocky promontory that towers over Kununurra, looks over a microcosm of what the early settlers hoped outback Australia would be like—lush green cane fields, orchards, and the blue waters of Lake Argyle in the distance.

The reality, however, lies beyond these surveyed and irrigated edges—in the harsh and dusty immensity of earth and sky.

Following pages: *A massive boab tree braces against the might of the Fitzroy River in full flood. Close relative of African and Madagascan baobabs, boabs are largely confined to Australia's northwest coast.*

Largest and most feared of all Australian creatures, a saltwater crocodile warms itself in the shallows of Cape York Peninsula's Shelburne Bay. "Salties," as these reptiles are called, can grow to more than 20 feet in length and can weigh well over a ton. Occasionally, they make a meal of an unwary human.

In the Jardine River of Cape York a saltie swims beneath water lily pads. An estimated 150,000 of these reptiles once lurked in the mangrove swamps and rivers of northern Australia, but hunting beginning in the 1940s whittled that number. Today, salties are protected, and their numbers are on the rise. An estimated 65,000 survive in the Northern Territory.

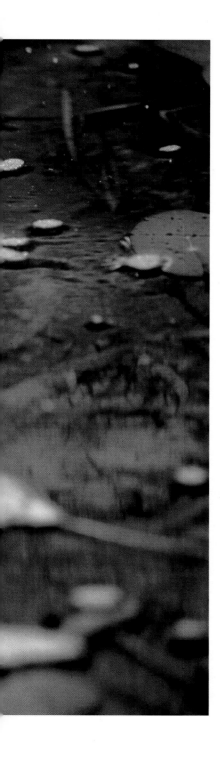

Vast and remote, the marshes of Cape York's Lakefield National Park conceal their own lost worlds. A termite mound rises from grassland that shelters a nest of magpie goose eggs. Scores of bird species call the park home. From April to November, after wet-season flooding, swamps and water holes that cover the lowlands shelter thousands of migratory birds.

Following pages: Like weather-worn tombstones, termite mounds pock charred earth of the Cape York Peninsula. Both fire and termites play life-giving roles in the area's ecology. Termites break down dead wood and grasses, while intense dry-season fires release nutrients. Monsoon rains will redraft the scene, creating a tropical fantasia.

Red-winged parrot perches on rain-battered spear grass stalks in the savanna near Nhulunbuy, a remote community in the ancient Aboriginal homeland known as Arnhem Land. A product of the wet season, spear grass can grow as much as 15 feet a month, but as the monsoons gather tempo, the grasses are slowly beaten down into a watery mat. Aborigines called these fiercest torrents bang-gereng—the knock'em down rains.

Following pages: Spiky barricade against the outside world, a dead mangrove on a lonely beach in the Northern Territory evokes the harshness of Australia's forbidding northern coast. Battered by tropical cyclones, washed by treacherous tides, steamed in tropical heat, and haunted by crocodiles, this ragged coast remains a wild frontier 60,000 years after the first Aborigines stepped ashore here.

by Frank Brennan, S.J.

The Aboriginal Struggle for Land, Life, and Culture

For decades European explorers had sailed past the coastline of the Great South Land. Meanwhile, Macassan sailors from the Indonesian archipelago made frequent visits to the northern shores of Australia, meeting and trading with the Aborigines. In 1770 Captain James Cook sailed up the east coast of Australia. He then went ashore on a small island in the Torres Strait, north of Cape York. In the name of His Majesty, the British King, he claimed possession of the continent he had sailed past and named the island Possession Island. In 1788 Captain Arthur Phillip established a penal colony at Sydney Cove, asserting British sovereignty over the east of the Australian continent. It could then be lawfully settled in the name of King George III.

The Aborigines were treated as if they had no rights to their traditional lands—lands that they had occupied and used for tens of thousands of years for hunting, camping, and ceremony. To European eyes, the Aborigines were nomadic hunters and gatherers who had no regard for the biblical injunction to fill the Earth and subdue it. They were not seen as owners of the land. Even Europeans who had some concern for the well-being of the Aborigines presumed that they could be moved from their traditional lands close to settlements. The Aborigines, settlers assumed, could hunt and camp just as happily on other land not required for European development.

The Aborigines enjoyed tens of thousands of years in splendid isolation and were spared foreign aggression until 1788. The continent held plenty of room and food for everyone. The Aboriginal population was probably fewer than one million spread throughout the entire continent. The Aborigines did not see themselves as one united people. Without a common foe there was no need for that. They had time to develop hundreds of languages and elaborate religious beliefs about their origins and relationships. Land was central to any group's identity and religious beliefs. The members of an Aboriginal group saw themselves as belonging to their land. While Europeans considered themselves the future owners of the land, Aborigines saw themselves as being owned by the land. Distinctive landforms were the story book of the activities of ancestral beings of the Dreamtime—the eternally present past. To the Aborigines dispossession meant much more than the loss of real estate. It meant the loss of their whole world of meaning.

As the frontier of European settlement expanded, the Aborigines were dispossessed of their traditional country. They often suffered the devastating effects of first contact, including smallpox and murder. Eventually, the British claimed sovereignty over the entire Australian continent, establishing six colonies. In London, the Secretary of State for Colonies issued periodic instructions urging the colonists to respect the Aborigines' rights to continuing use and occupation of their hunting and camping grounds. But the colonists' greed and convenience always took precedence over the claims of the Aborigines.

Colonial expansion continued into the remotest regions of the continent. The settlers claimed that they were simply occupying land that was *terra nullius,* land belonging to nobody. The local colonial authorities, who were a world away from their masters in London, permitted settlers to take over vast tracts of land for farming and grazing. The colonies were moving toward self-government, and the new landholders were most unsympathetic to any directives from Sydney or London that urged them to accommodate the Aborigines. They were a threat to the sheep, cattle, and families of the settlers. The lands being claimed for sheep runs were vast areas in the style of American ranches. Land grants half the size of Wales were incomprehensible to civil servants sitting at their desks in London. They had, however, humanitarian concern for the well-being of the natives. Secretary of State Henry Grey, the third Earl Grey, wrote to the Governor of New South Wales in 1848:

> It should be generally understood that Leases granted for this purpose give the grantees only an exclusive right of pasturage for their cattle, and of cultivating such Land as they may require within

the large limits thus assigned to them, but that these Leases are not intended to deprive the Natives of their former right to hunt over these Districts, or to wander over them in search of subsistence, in the manner to which they have been heretofore accustomed, from the spontaneous produce of the soil except over land actually cultivated or fenced in for that purpose.

On the frontier massacres occurred, and the dispossession continued. While many coastal areas were settled by the newcomers, especially in the south, where the weather was more appealing to Europeans, the remoter regions and the northern areas remained untouched by them for another hundred years. The hot climate and the unproductive soil provided the Aborigines in these parts with a shield from the colonizers. Australia's other indigenous people, the Torres Strait Islanders, did not experience European settlement until the arrival of the London Missionary Society in the 1870s, the islands having been included in the colony of Queensland in 1869. On the mainland a few Aboriginal tribes were spared any sustained European contact until well into this century. The Yolngu people in Arnhem Land had their first contact with the arrival of Methodist missionaries in 1935. No matter how late the contact came, however, the indigenous people of Australia were treated as if they had no rights to their land.

In 1901 the six colonies formed a federation, the Commonwealth of Australia. A constitution listed the powers of the Commonwealth Parliament, the equivalent of the U.S. Congress, leaving all other legislative powers to the states. The Commonwealth Parliament did not have power to make laws with respect to Aborigines. The states maintained sole power in relation to Aborigines. Land issues were also the exclusive concern of the states. There was no equivalent provision to one in the United States Constitution that empowers Congress to regulate commerce with Indian tribes. There were no treaties with the Aborigines. Though reserves of public land were set aside for Aborigines, these reserves were governed by state authorities. The reserves were public land that could be dedicated to other purposes by state governments without compensating or consulting with the Aborigines. And they could be moved to other places at the state's convenience.

It was not until the 1960s that Aborigines and their supporters were heard on the streets and on the airwaves campaigning for civil rights and land rights. Much of the attention focused on the Northern Territory. Unlike the states of Australia, the territory was under federal control. Much of it was still inhabited only by Aborigines. In 1963 the Yolngu people of Arnhem Land, who had tolerated the presence of a few Methodist missionaries for some 30 years, were informed that the national government was going to allow a Swiss consortium to mine bauxite on their traditional lands. The Aborigines objected strongly, and, with assistance from the missionaries, drafted petitions to the Commonwealth Parliament. The Yolngu demanded that they be consulted and that no arrangements be made with any company that would destroy their livelihood and independence. Their pleas fell on deaf ears, and they decided to claim their land rights in court.

The social policies affecting Aborigines were starting to change. There had been many state-implemented race-based laws and policies that treated Aborigines differently from other people. Aborigines had been banned from consuming alcohol. They had been paid low wages on cattle stations. Aborigines under the age of 21 had been automatically treated as wards of the state. Children, especially those of mixed descent, were often separated from their parents and brought up in institutions run by government or churches. These children became known as the "stolen generations." Some of these policies were benignly administered in a protective way, but often they were racist. When Aborigines pushed their claim for equal wages on cattle stations, the European owners warned that equal wages would mean fewer jobs for Aborigines. The cattle station owners were not prepared to allow Aboriginal families to stay on the stations unless family members were employed. So the benign policy of equal wages resulted in even more Aborigines having to leave their traditional country. Dispossession and dislocation continued.

In 1967 the Australian people voted overwhelmingly to amend the constitution so that the Commonwealth Parliament would have power to make laws with respect to Aborigines throughout the nation and not only in Commonwealth territories. The issue of Aboriginal rights was no longer just a domestic issue of concern only to state governments. It was now a national issue, with international ramifications. The national government, however, suspecting that Aboriginal claims to land were Communist inspired, proceeded very cautiously. The government would not even grant the Aborigines a lease over eight square miles of their traditional country at Lord Vestey's Wave Hill Station lest this be a precedent for other claims and encourage the Aborigines to set up permanent facilities on the land.

In 1971 the Yolngu people from Arnhem Land who had opposed bauxite mining lost their land-rights claim in the Northern Territory court. The judge decided that British common law did not recognize any communal interests in land and that any Aboriginal rights to land would have been extinguished by the assertion of sovereignty by the British authorities at the time of their arrival and settlement.

During the election year of 1972 Aborigines set up a tent embassy outside Parliament House in Canberra. The Australian Labor Party's Gough Whitlam, Leader of the Opposition, pledged his party to granting land rights if elected. After the election the Whitlam government held an inquiry into Aboriginal land rights and drafted a federal law for the Northern Territory. This government, which lasted only three years, also passed through Parliament the Racial Discrimination Act. That act banned state governments and parliaments from acting in a racially discriminatory way. This new law was to become the Aboriginal bill of rights because it would strike down any law or policy of state governments that singled out Aborigines for special treatment without their consent. This would mean an end to the old laws and policies that discriminated against Aborigines. Aborigines could now go to court when they could not win popular support for their rights from politicians. In 1977 the Northern Territory's land-rights law went into effect, and some states also passed laws allowing the governments to grant land title to Aboriginal communities. The states of Queensland and Western Australia, covering the northern parts of Australia, were very slow to respond.

Queensland was host for the Commonwealth Games in 1982. These games are a mini-Olympics in which countries from the British Commonwealth of Nations compete. The international spotlight turned on Queensland's treatment of indigenous people when Eddie Mabo, a Torres Strait Islander, sued the state of Queensland in the High Court of Australia, claiming land rights on his traditional island of Mer. This was the first time Australia's highest court had been asked to consider whether indigenous people had any surviving rights to land that was theirs at the time of colonization. The Queensland government attempted to short circuit the court proceedings by passing a law through the Queensland parliament. That law

declared retrospectively that any native title rights had been extinguished without compensation in 1879 when the Torres Strait islands were made part of Queensland. The High Court struck down this state law because it was inconsistent with the Racial Discrimination Act.

In 1988 Australia celebrated its bicentennial. But the political question was: the bicentennial of what? The foundation of the nation did not occur in 1788; that did not take place until 1901. It was not the date of British sovereignty over the whole continent, but only over the eastern half. Aborigines said 1988 was the bicentennial of the commencement of their dispossession. Aboriginal claims for land rights and self-determination were heard more loudly and more clearly by Australians during this year of celebration. Indeed, it became a year of soul-searching about national identity.

In 1992 Eddie Mabo and his fellow Torres Strait Islanders won their claim for land rights in the High Court. It ruled that Australian common law recognized the native title of indigenous people. The native title rights survived until they were taken away by government's granting the land to someone else. But the government would have to respect Aboriginal land rights in the same way as any other land owner's rights.

The Mabo decision gave Aborigines real bargaining power in the political process. Thirty-six percent of the Australian landmass was still "vacant crown land" or "Aboriginal reserve" where native title could still exist. If mining companies wanted access to that land for exploration or development, they had to act in a non-discriminatory way toward any native title holders. But there was no register of native title holders. The miners did not know with whom to deal, and they thought it unfair that they bear the cost of ascertaining the identity and claims of native title holders. The Australian government and key Aboriginal leaders negotiated a solution that was then made law: All actions taken on land since the Racial Discrimination Act would be valid only if compensation was paid when there had been interference with native title rights. If mining companies in future wanted access to land subject to native title claim, they would need to negotiate with the claimant.

One matter remained unresolved: Could native title survive in some form on cattle stations when a "pastoral lease" had been granted with the understanding that Aborigines would have access to the land for hunting, fishing, camping, and ceremony? A pastoral lease was a special title over a vast area of land that permitted the grazing of cattle but did not grant ownership of the land. In 1996 the High Court ruled in favor of the Wik peoples from Cape York. The Wik claimed ongoing native title rights on land that had been subject to pastoral lease. The mining industry was perturbed because pastoral leases cover another 42 percent of the continent. The effect of the decision was that future mining activity on 78 percent of the continent (the 42 percent pastoral lease land and 36 percent vacant crown land or Aboriginal reserve) could not proceed unless there was first an assessment made of native title.

The 1993 Native Title Act set up the machinery for dealing with native title. It was proposed by Paul Keating, who, as prime minister, placed great emphasis on including Aborigines in the consultations. Keating appreciated the need for the country to reach a just and lasting agreement with the indigenous leadership after two centuries of terra nullius. The Keating government readily acknowledged that most Aborigines could never establish a native title claim because they had been dispossessed of their land or lost all contact and association with the land. A land fund administered by indigenous Australians to allow the purchase of land on the open market was set up as some compensation for all that had been lost.

In 1998 the government had to deal with the effects of the High Court's Wik decision. Prime Minister John Howard proposed changes to the Native Title Act that wound back the gains that Aborigines had made under Paul Keating's laws. The Howard government was sympathetic to business interests, having thought that the previous Keating government and the High Court had gone too far in accommodating Aboriginal claims. The Howard government thought that too much Aboriginal policy had been moved on to the national stage and should be returned to the states. The Native Title Act has now been amended so that states can set up their own tribunals for the determination of native title claims. States can also reduce the Aboriginal right to negotiate with mining companies on pastoral leases. The changes made by the Howard government did not have the support of the indigenous leaders.

The Aboriginal campaign for rights, recognition, and reconciliation has broadened beyond the issues of land rights. The topic of land rights is not just about the preservation of culture and identity: It is also about political and economic power in Australian society. Many Aborigines want to manage their own affairs on their traditional lands in the way that the Indian tribes do on their reservations in the United States. There it is readily accepted that tribes will maintain some jurisdiction over law and order on tribal land and some economic advantages such as the power to run casinos or to conduct mining. Many Australians, however, still think that equality demands that Aborigines be subject to the same law on their land as any other Australians.

Aborigines want the Australian Parliament to apologize for past government policies that separated so many Aboriginal children from their families and their lands. While Aborigines over the last 30 years have won the battle against adverse legal discrimination, they have not yet won the hearts and minds of other Australians about their entitlements to special recognition as the indigenous people of the continent. Though there is now broad support for giving Aborigines some favorable mention in the constitution, there is no agreement about the constitutional recognition of indigenous rights. During the 1988 bicentennial, the Aborigines issued the Barunga Statement. It now hangs in the parliament building in Canberra. They called on the Commonwealth Parliament "to negotiate with us a Treaty or Compact recognising our prior ownership, continued occupation and sovereignty and affirming our human rights and freedoms." When the eyes of the world turn to Sydney during the Olympic Games in the year 2000, that treaty will still be only a dream. All social indicators will still place Aborigines on the bottom of the social ladder. Many of them will still be fringe-dwellers in the Great South Land that has been their country for tens of thousands of years.

Australians are still undecided about the terms of recognition and equality for Aborigines who have maintained connection with their traditional lands and culture despite two centuries of dispossession and assimilation. In 1996, marking the 20th anniversary of Australia's recognition of his people's land rights, Mr. Galarrwuy Yunupingu, Chairman of the Northern Land Council in the Northern Territory, said to his people: "This land is something that is always yours; it doesn't matter what nature or politics do to change it. We believe the land is all life. So it comes to us that we are part of the land and the land is part of us."

The Aboriginal struggle to put right the wrongs of the past continues.

Sanctified by pungent fumes from the smoldering leaves of a conkerberry bush, a newborn named Veronica receives a traditional Aboriginal baptism as her grandmother, Rita Sturt, passes her over a ritual fire. The smoke is believed to clear an infant's chest and head and launch the baby into a healthy life.

Handprints on a cliff near Wyndham evoke the 2,000 generations of Aborigines who dwelled in the Kimberley's labyrinthine canyons and gorges. Stencils were made by spraying a mouthful of pigment over the artist's hand. Millennia of spear sharpening left gouges and grooves in the sandstone. Thousands of such rock art galleries lie scattered throughout the far north.

*Aboriginal dancers daubed with clay
and ocher prepare for a tribal
corroboree, or ceremonial dance,
near Derby in the Kimberley. The
139,000-square-mile wilderness of
ancient gorges and mountain ranges
in Western Australia's remote northwest frontier remains a stronghold of
Aboriginal culture and rock art.*

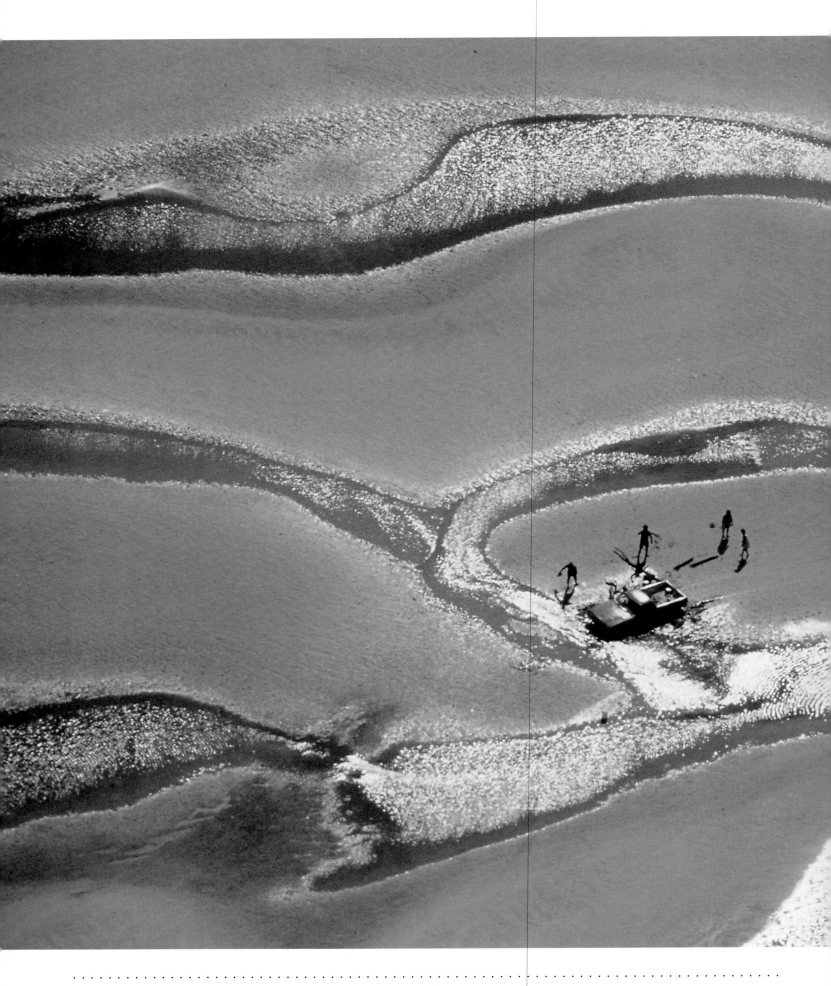

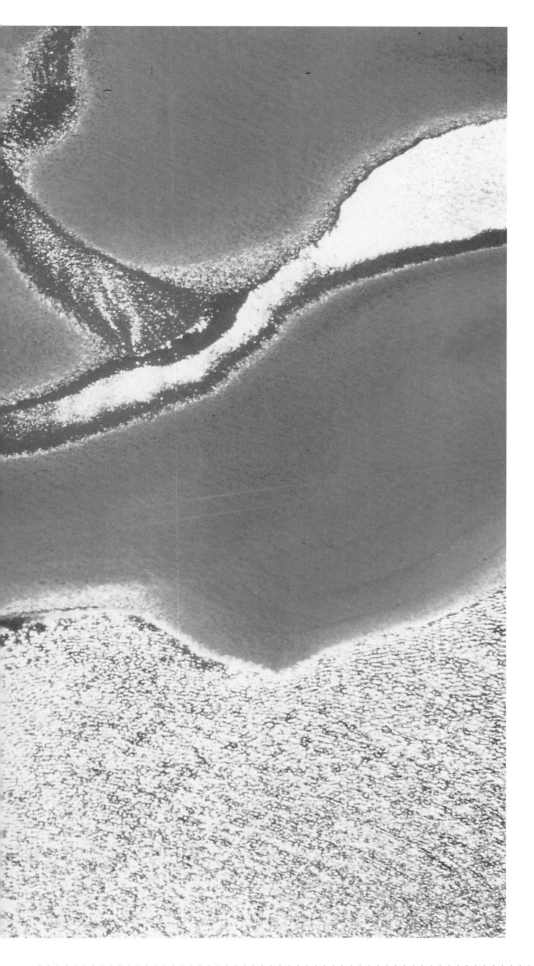

Bogged in beach sand, stranded travelers on Queensland's Cape York Peninsula signal a passing light plane. The pilot radioed for help, and rescuers from a nearby Aboriginal community winched the truck out before high tide swamped it. Monsoons, crocodiles, and incredible isolation can make travel in Australia's far north an exhilarating adventure—or a trap for the unwary.

Following pages: Master of a 610,000-acre cattle station on the Cape York Peninsula of Queensland, John Fraser poses with his son and grandchildren in front of their homestead. In addition to running 4,000 cattle, Fraser guides hunts for feral bulls and wild pigs. The horns of a rogue bull and trophy tusks line the hood of his battered Land Rover.

Offbeat humor pervades the outback, where many conveniences must be built by hand. Jackaroos at Drysdale River Station joke that they have to keep the telephone in the fridge so that it doesn't melt. Phones replaced static-filled radio chat sessions in the Kimberley only about 20 years ago.

Isolation and rugged individualism have bred a unique and whimsical inventiveness in the Australian bush. At Ellenbrae Station, in the heart of the Kimberley, New Age residents built an outdoor tub and plumbing into the massive trunk of an old boab tree. In fact, the boab remains a traditional source of water in the Kimberley bush.

Following pages: *John Koeyers and his children unwind in the homesteader's Drysdale River Station auto-repair shop and playroom— his garage. Drysdale's isolation, more than 200 air miles from the nearest town, means that the children receive their education through the School of the Air, with lessons beamed daily by radio from Derby.*

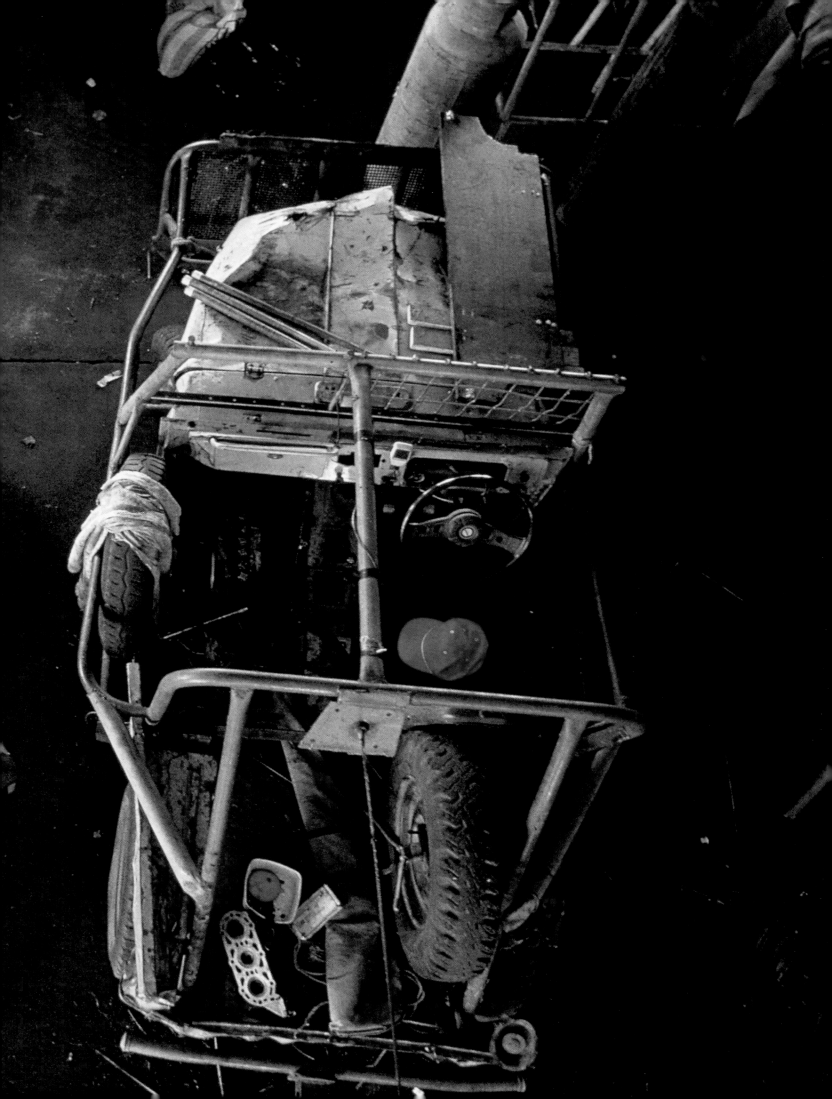

Contestants and spectactors gather around a massive boab tree at a demolition derby in the Western Australia town of Derby. The competition forms part of the Boab Annual Festival, which runs for two weeks each July in the town on the west Kimberley coast.

Weary but watchful, a jockey at a race in Broome cradles his saddle as he studies the proceedings. Race meetings take place each June and July in the old pearling port on the Indian Ocean.

Ready to ride, an Aboriginal stock-man awaits his turn during a Kim-berley Championship Rodeo. Already masters of outback bush craft, by the turn of the century Aborigines had earned renown as the finest riders and wranglers on the range despite never having seen horses or cattle until the arrival of Europeans.

Cooling water eases the heat at an annual race meeting in Broome. Tourism based on its beaches grows in the rambunctious old pearling port, but its brawling saloons and hard-drinking stockmen keep a frontier flavor alive.

Beef for the "barbie" fills a truck bed at a cattle station near Halls Creek in the Kimberley. Served outback style—in huge blood red chunks—the beef will feed the crew during the annual roundup. Stations in the Kimberley average more than half a million wild acres. Helicopters often drive cattle into pens for shipment to market.

Following pages: *Largest diamond producer in the world, the secluded Argyle Diamond Mine glows pink in a Kimberley sunset. Each year some 38 million carats of raw diamonds— more than one third of the world's total production—come from this well-guarded pit in the Ragged Ranges. The world's sole reliable source of intense pink diamonds, the Argyle produces only a handful of the ultrarare stones each year.*

CHAPTER TWO

The Outback

Explorer Charles Sturt headed into the burning deserts in South Australia in 1830, optimistically towing a boat behind him. Sturt and his party had ventured into the outback to answer once and for all one of the Victorian era's burning geographical questions: Does Australia have an inland sea? Visions of water and fertile plains in the heart of their country had been tugging at Australian imaginations since the first explorers crossed the Blue Mountains, 75 miles west of Sydney, in 1813.

Sturt's trek was a journey into hell. For months he and his men were tormented by thirst, flies, dust, and temperatures that soared to more than 150 degrees before winter rains finally came and offered some relief. Sturt was eventually forced back, his sadly useless boat abandoned like a forlorn hope.

Determined to succeed, Sturt mounted another expedition in 1844. A young John MacDouall Stuart went along on that expedition. It taught him a lot about travel in the harsh outback and fired his own enthusiasm to find the elusive watery heartland. Fifteen years later, on a desolate hill in what he believed to be the exact center of the continent, he laconically noted in his journal:

Took Kekwick and the flag, and went to the top of the mount, but found it to be much higher and more difficult of ascent than I anticipated. After a deal of labour, slips and knocks, we at last arrived on the top.... Built a large cone of stones, in the centre of which I placed a pole with the British flag nailed to it. Near the top of the cone I placed a small bottle, in which there is a slip of paper, with our signatures to it, stating by whom

it was raised. We then gave three hearty cheers for the flag, the emblem of civil and religious liberty, and may it be a sign to the natives that the dawn of liberty, civilisation and Christianity is about to break upon them. We can see no water from the top.

Imagine that lonely scene. Two sunburned explorers on a stony hilltop surrounded by a dusty immensity of earth and sky that seemed to stretch for more than a thousand miles in every direction, their dry-throated hurrahs swallowed up in the profound outback stillness.

The truth was slowly dawning. Stuart had named the stony hilltop Central Mount Sturt, after his mentor, during an expedition in 1860. In 1861 he returned. This time he pressed on toward the top end of the continent. Instead of an inland sea and a fertile heartland, there was only outback: Arid plains dotted with spinifex, vast stretches of burning sand dunes, and miles upon miles of dazzling salt flats.

Stuart crossed the continent successfully, but he returned in 1862 a broken man. His body was wracked with scurvy, and he was nearly blind from months of glare, flies, and dust. His health irretrievably ruined, he returned to London and died three years later.

Today the hilltop on which Stuart and Kekwick hoisted the Union Jack has been renamed Central Mount Stuart in honor of his accomplishments. It lies just off the lonely Stuart Highway, Australia's main outback route, which crosses the continent in the explorer's footsteps. Stuart was a tad off the mark, though, in his reckoning when he placed his hilltop in the center of Australia; today's navigational aids put the geographical center of the continent about 250 miles south, close to Alice Springs. With the exception of the long strip of asphalt stretching from horizon to horizon, little has changed out here since Stuart's time.

A couple of years ago I bicycled 600 miles of the lonely Stuart Highway, from Tennant Creek north to Darwin. I used to think of the great South Australian explorer as I set up my little camps in the fragrant bush beneath the blaze of outback stars. Although I was on a bicycle and had the happy advantage of covering a hundred miles a day on a mapped highway, our days had a lot in common. Like the early explorers I had to rise before dawn to take advantage of the relative morning cool, then find a patch of shade by ten o'clock to escape the outback's blinding midday heat, dozing away the motionless hours while flies hummed overhead. And in the evenings, as I watched a blood red sun sink into the timeless scrub, I rationed out my stale warm water for the next day's ride and longed for a cool drink. Obviously I had it a lot easier than Stuart and his colleagues: At least I knew where I was and what lay ahead. But even with the benefit of road maps, satellite photos, and views from the windows of a plane passing over the continent at 37,000 feet, the sheer size, harshness, and emptiness of outback Australia is hard to comprehend.

How big is it? Well, I estimate that the outback covers more than 70 percent of the continent, an area of more than two million square miles. But numbers hardly do it justice. Put it another way: You could lose Texas out there with barely a ripple. Western Australia alone is about the size of India. Outback doctors and priests and magistrates get about in light aircraft, and their "local" territories may be larger than the whole of the United Kingdom. Ranchers measure their properties—they call them stations—by the square mile, or even by the hundreds of square miles. The world's biggest cattle station is in South Australia: Anna Creek, all 7 million plus acres of it, or about 12,000 square miles, perched on the edge of the vast Simpson Desert. Anna Creek is run by the Kidman family, one of Australia's oldest grazing

dynasties. The Kidmans lease several other multi-million-acre spreads in the area for a total of about 45,000 square miles. For sheer size that is like owning Pennsylvania. It makes the Kidmans *one* of outback Australia's biggest landowners.

Children growing up on these lonely stations attend school by radio, since the nearest town may be several hours drive away. And they grow up fast. I've ridden down a rough track on a sheep station in central Queensland in a Land Cruiser steered by a three-year-old girl who was sitting on her father's lap, getting practice. And she was a good, assertive driver, too. "You never know, out here, one of us adults might be injured and she might be the only one able to go off for help," he explained. Confidence and competence are doubly important qualities out here. In addition to horses, graziers use light aircraft to look over their properties or go to town, and they round up their livestock with helicopters.

Until 1928 the incredible isolation of Australia's outback meant that anyone who lived out on the remote stations or Aboriginal communities had little or no access to medical facilities. Life in the bush is hard and often dangerous, and those who were unlucky enough to become seriously ill or injured could expect to wait many days for a doctor to come up a rough bush track by pack horse or camel. That is, if a doctor was available.

It took the twin 20th-century miracles of radio and airplane, and a compassionate Presbyterian missionary named John Flynn, to bring medicine to the bush. In 1912 Flynn established the first hospital in the outback, in the remote South Australian town of Oodnadatta. But there was still no way for many outback dwellers to reach the hospital or to alert doctors to any medical crisis in the bush. In 1927 an electrical engineer named Alfred Traeger invented a simple but effective pedal-powered radio transmitter that would allow people living on lonely outback stations to send messages to towns or neighbors up to 300 miles away. This device, coupled with larger aircraft capable of transporting stretcher-bound patients, opened the door to aerial medical service.

The first base opened in 1928, in Cloncurry, an old mining town in Queensland's rugged northwest that by then had become a stop for the Queensland & Northern Territory Aerial Service (Qantas). The medical service was based out of the Qantas aerodrome and leased its planes and pilots to ferry doctors to their outback patients. The first call was to an injured stockman near Julia Creek, about 80 miles east of the new base.

As word spread, other outback regions asked to have an aerial medical service as well. The Presbyterian Church couldn't afford to expand the operation, and in 1934 a nonprofit organization—the Australian Aerial Medical Service—was formed to serve the outback. Today, the organization, called the Royal Flying Doctor Service, is one of Australia's proudest and most remarkable traditions. There are 20 RFDS bases scattered around the country. Dentists, specialists, physiotherapists, and psychologists make the rounds of outback communities. Dashes to outlying stations and dramatic evacuations on isolated dirt strips are still a big part of life in the RFDS, but it performs a comprehensive range of less heralded medical services as well. It runs regular medical clinics at distant stations and Aboriginal communities, offering immunizations and checkups. Even in the outback, anyone in Australia is now no more than about two hours from emergency medical assistance.

Like medical service, mail delivery must cope with the enormous distances in the outback. The world's longest mail run leaves Port Augusta, in South Australia, at 8:30 every Saturday morning. It is a two-day, 28-stop marathon by light aircraft to isolated stations and settlements scattered for hundreds of miles along the Strezleki and Birdsville Tracks.

On Australia's vast cattle and sheep stations themselves, four-wheel drives assigned to checking the water holes clock up 60,000 miles a year—without ever leaving the property. Even the towns are huge. Mount Isa, a silver- and lead-mining town of 22,000 in northwest Queensland, is the world's biggest municipality. It sprawls over an area almost the size of Switzerland.

Everything is oversize out here. To protect their sheep from dingoes, outback graziers built the longest fence in the world, 3,307 miles from Queensland's Darling Downs to South Australia's cliff-lined coast on the Great

Australian Bight—a thousand miles longer than the Great Wall of China. The trucks that hammer down empty outback highways are road trains, which can weigh more than 140 tons and haul three trailers. Allow at least a mile of open highway to pass one. Fortunately, long stretches of straight open highway are fairly easy to find. The longest of these is on the Eyre Highway, between Balladonia station and the lonely Caiguna roadhouse. It runs dead straight for 53 empty miles.

Surprisingly, given its immense size, Australia's outback is a little hard to delineate on a map. Ask around, as I did on a 10,000-mile bicycle trek around Australia, and you'll soon find that no two Australians can agree on exactly where the outback starts. As a rule of thumb, it's anywhere west of the Great Dividing Range, the rugged spine of mountains than runs along Australia's eastern seaboard, and covers the vast stretch of open land across the continent to the Indian Ocean. It includes the wide-open arid grazing lands in western Queensland and New South Wales—the mythical outback Australia of "Waltzing Matilda" and the Flying Doctor Service and Big Jackie Howe, the champion shearer who sheared 321 sheep one day at Alice Downs Station in 1892. It is also the harsh red center, near Alice Springs, with its colorful history of Afghan camel drivers, the Overland Telegraph line, and the haunting spectacle of Uluru. It is the blinding white salt pans and inhospitable wastelands of South Australia, where Burke and Wills perished in 1861. It is the saltbush and mallee scrub along the Murray-Darling Rivers and the mining town of Broken Hill. And it is the vast and silent desert in Western Australia, where the prospector Lasseter perished while trying to find his way back to his fabulous lost gold strike.

Nevertheless, a traveler can amble down thousands of miles of lonely bush tracks, through endless harsh and lonely landscapes, without ever reaching the outback. In nine months of hard riding, through lonely outback wastes, from the gulf savanna in the north to the waterless expanses of the Nullarbor Plain in the south, I never heard anyone tell me that, yes, you are now in the outback. The outback was farther out still, somewhere beyond the next elusive—and usually heat-warped—horizon. That's because to most Australians the outback is a sort of state of grace, a nation's soul. Part myth and part ballad, it can't be fettered by the here and now, or reached in any four-wheel drive. It is a sort of rootless, ornery freedom, of frayed cuffs and laconic humor and the swag, the canvas bedroll slung over the shoulders of drifters roving the open country looking for work, the next meal or anything else that might turn up. "The Australian swag," declared writer Henry Lawson, "was born of Australia and no other land—of the Great Lone Land of magnificent distances and bright heat; the land of self-reliance, and never-give-in, and help-your-mate. The grave of many of the world's tragedies and comedies—royal and otherwise. The land where a man out of employment might shoulder his swag in Adelaide and take the track, and years later walk into a hut on the Gulf, or never be heard of any more, or a body be found in the bush and buried by the mounted police, or never found and never buried—what does it matter?"

Whatever it is and wherever it is, the outback is certainly no place for the fainthearted. Out here is some of the toughest and most inhospitable terrain in the world—the Simpson Desert, the Gibson Desert, the Great Victoria Desert, the Great Sandy Desert, Sturt Stony Desert, and the Tanami Desert, to name a few of the better known wastelands. There are vast, dusty, anonymous plains dotted with saltbush or covered with tangled mallee scrub—a gnarled and stunted species of euca-lypt—or, farther north, mile upon mile of spinifex, a prickly type of clump grass that looks like so many millions of huddled porcupines in the distance. Yes, some of the cattle and sheep stations out here might be the size of small European countries or American states, but the browse is so lean that it can take more than 50 acres to support a single animal. Droughts are frequent and can last for years. The dramatic storms that break the droughts can leave vast areas flooded for weeks at a time. The blinding summer heat and roasting northerly winds are almost beyond belief to anyone who has never experienced them.

"At noon I took a thermometer, graduated to 127°, out of my box and observed that the mercury was up to 125°," wrote an amazed Capt. Charles Sturt on his expedition in 1844. "Thinking that it had been unduly influenced, I put it in the fork of a tree close to me, sheltered alike from the wind and the sun. In this position I went to examine it about an hour afterwards, when I found that the mercury had risen to the top of the instrument, and that its further expansion had burst the bulb, a circumstance that I believe no traveller has ever before had to record."

The journals of most of the early European explorers are punctuated with starvation, scurvy, thirst, desperation, sunstroke and blindness. For all their misery and torment, Sturt and his crew were lucky. Most of them survived, staggering into Adelaide looking like living skeletons, after having long been given up for dead. Less fortunate was the Prussian explorer, Ludwig Leichhardt, who set off in 1848 from Roma, Queensland, on an attempt to be the first to cross the heart of the continent east to west. His entire party vanished. Many others owed their lives to Aborigines, to whom these seemingly hostile wastes were a comfortable home.

The classic symbol of the Australian outback is the hypnotically beautiful monolith known as Uluru—formerly Ayers Rock—in the Northern Territory. It rises abruptly almost 1,200 feet above the desert at the heart of the continent, throwing the surrounding flatness and desolation into hauntingly sharp relief. Uluru—the name means "great pebble" in the Pitjantjatjara language—is a single chunk of hardened sandstone more than 600 million years old.

Eons of wind, rain, and shifting seasons exposed it, wearing away the softer earth around it. Geologists believe that only the top 10 percent of Uluru is visible. Much more is still buried under the desert. Even so, it is a six-mile hike all the way around the base of this "great pebble." This excursion is far more than merely a scenic approach to a geologic marvel, with up-close looks at its ancient striated flanks, sculpted gullies, and overhangs, and the rioting wildflowers that spring up at its base thanks to runoff rains. Uluru is an epicenter of Aboriginal spiritual life, and the path circling it is a journey into a Dreamtime culture with ancient roots.

Aboriginal spiritual life revolves around ancestral spirit beings, which dwelled on Earth during a prehistoric

Dreamtime era before human beings were created. These beings originally had human form, but later changed into other creatures—magpies, snakes, wallabies, and caterpillars. As they wandered the continent in search of food and water, they fashioned the landscape and, over time, became the ancestors of all living things. The paths they followed in their time on Earth are full of power and are celebrated in elaborate cycles of song, ritual, and painting. These activities keep alive many forms of ancient wisdom, such as advising hunters when and where to search for game and how to find water in the dry years, and giving details about the origins of complex kinship and marriage customs. Many of these powerful, invisible Aboriginal pathways intersect at Uluru—such as those of Mala, the hare wallaby; Kuniya, the python; and Kiru, the viper—giving this haunting desert monolith immense spiritual significance. The sculpted crevices and overhangs around its base are filled with rock paintings and engravings dating back thousands of years.

Many of these are sacred sites—some set aside strictly for women, others set aside strictly for men—and today's visitors to Uluru are expected to respect these ancient Aboriginal customs. While specific spiritual aspects of the rock remain closely guarded secrets known only to the initiated, the grandeur and mystique of Uluru are as obvious as the rock itself.

It is one of the most recognized Australian icons in the world and the centerpiece of 327,570-acre Uluru-Kata Tjuta National Park, about 200 miles southwest of Alice Springs. Australia formally returned Uluru to the Aborigines in 1985, and they leased it back to the government for 99 years as a national park, with Aborigines taking a majority of seats on the park's board of directors. The Lasseter Highway, which only a few years ago was a dirt track, is now a smoothly paved two-lane highway, and the airstrip, near a luxury resort at Yulara, handles daily jet traffic from most of Australia's cities. Tourists come to wonder and to be moved—to admire the play of light and shadow on the rock's grooved face, and to marvel at the way it subtly shifts colors as the sun arches through the sky. Over the course of a day Uluru grades from pale, desert pink through a spectrum of mauves and coppery browns, and finishes, in the dying rays of an outback sunset, in a fiery and luminous crimson.

Oddly, all this magnificence was lost on the first European to visit Uluru back in 1873. He was a singularly unimaginative surveyor named William Gosse whose laconic journal entry that night remarks that he had climbed "a high hill east of Mount Olga, which I named Ayers Rock...."

But Gosse did start a tradition. About two-thirds of today's visitors make the same climb up the incredibly steep and exposed flank of the rock. This hike is only for those with a good head for heights and strong thighs. I did it in 1989, and it left my legs feeling like jelly. The heart-stopping descent left blisters on my toes from being jammed into the ends of my boots. I wouldn't do it again, although not because it was so strenuous. Over the years the local Aborigines have politely let it be known that the route the tourists use to climb the rock follows a spiritual track, and that they would very much prefer visitors to admire Uluru from its base.

As custodians of this ancient marvel, the Aborigines are deeply saddened when a visitor is injured on the climb. This is an event that occurs about once a year, usually from heart attacks or something silly like chasing a windblown hat over an exposed ledge. For a time the park service tried putting white crosses at the base of Uluru to discourage the old and unfit. The only result was that a lot of fat, middle-aged men began mugging for the camera in front of these somber warnings—and then starting up the rock anyway. And so the crosses were removed. So far the Aborigines have shown a remarkable tolerance for tourists' foibles and have not yet banned the climb, although they are considering it.

The Aboriginal owners are more guarded about the jumble of 36 enormous sandstone domes known as Kata Tjuta—the name means "many heads"—that are about 20 miles west of Uluru. Tourists to this sacred spot—which for visual spectacle is as least as good as Uluru—are restricted to just a couple of short trails. Like Uluru, this ancient range was hewn out of a single Precambrian sandstone block. It used to be known to European travelers as the Olgas. Explorer Ernest Giles, who camped here in 1872, christened them in honor of Queen Olga of Württemberg. "The appearance of Mt Olga from this camp is truly wonderful," he wrote. "It displayed to our astonished eyes rounded minarets, giant cupolas and monstrous domes. They have stood as huge memorials from the ancient times of earth, for ages, countless eons of ages since creation first had birth. Time, the old, the dim magician, has ineffectually labored here...Mount Olga has remained as it was born."

In the red heart of Australia about 200 miles northeast of Uluru, Alice Springs, affectionately known as "the Alice," nestles in the craggy Macdonnell Ranges. More than any other town, it has come to symbolize the rough-and-ready Aussie outback. As Uluru is a crossroads of Aboriginal song lines, so the town of Alice Springs is the hub of modern outback legends, myths, and creation stories. The Alice started out as a relay station for the Overland Telegraph—aptly nicknamed "the singing string"—which passed through here in 1872 and connected Australia, via Java, Singapore, and India, with London.

Over the years a dusty settlement sprang up around the telegraph station, serving as a sort of staging post for stockmen, prospectors, telegraph men, and camel drivers heading north or into the vast western deserts. In the early days and up until 1933, the settlement was called Stuart, after the outback explorer who passed near here in 1860. It was the year-round spring out by the telegraph station, two miles north of town, that was named Alice, in honor of Alice Todd, wife of Sir Charles Todd, the South Australian postmaster general who supervised the building of the Overland Telegraph.

Hardly anyone outside Australia had ever even heard of the place until 1950, when Nevil Shute's best-selling *A Town Like Alice* put the rough outback town on the world's literary map. Although it is much larger now—at around 30,000 residents—the Alice retains its frontier rawness: "a grid of scorching streets where men in long white socks were forever getting in and out of Land Cruisers," wrote English travel writer Bruce Chatwin, who visited Alice Springs in 1986. Residents are mostly geologists, drill rig operators, railway workers, or jackaroos in from one of the stations. Although it rates high on the tourist map, Alice Springs still earns most of its keep from mining, oil, cattle, and transport. There's a modest export industry in shipping wild camels to the Middle East, and even a winery on the outskirts of town.

This is a restless hard-drinking oasis of transients and tourists, known for such rowdy events as its camel races and the riotous Henley-on-Todd boat regatta in which competitors carry their boats down the dusty bed of the Todd River. The Alice Springs rodeo is one of the most respected on the Australian circuit. But behind all the blokey gaiety and the cavalcade of motels, fast-food joints, tacky souvenir shops, and travel agents touting excursions to Uluru and Kings Canyon is a sense of a smoldering, hard-boiled little town. Its society of rednecks, drunks, drifters, and the sad spectacle of outcast Aborigines living in squalor along the riverbank suggest a not-too-pretty raffishness just below the surface. Few people get sentimental about Alice Springs. It is what it always has been—a springboard to someplace else, somewhere over the horizon: the outback.

Every Tuesday and Friday, in the early afternoon, one of Australia's most romantic trains leaves the Alice on a 966-mile journey south through the desert and mulga scrub to Adelaide. The train is known affectionately as the *Ghan*, named in honor of the tough Afghan camel drivers who, together with their pack animals, kept the remote desert town supplied and were the unsung heroes of Australia's outback exploration.

Camels are not native to Australia, but they are ideal for traveling in the outback. Their broad, soft feet do not sink in sandy soils the way horses hoofs do; they could thrive on tough desert scrub; carry enormous loads; and, of course, they are famed for their abilities to travel long distances between water holes. A few experimental camels were imported as early as the 1840s, but it wasn't until the Victorian government bought 25 camels for the Burke and Wills expedition, in 1860, that the possibilities of using these ships of the desert to open up the outback began to be understood.

In 1866 South Australian pastoralist Thomas Elder imported 120 camels and began breeding them at his Beltana Station. Thousands more were imported. Within a few years and well into the 1930s, camel trains and their Afghan handlers were the mainstays of outback transportation. Some settlements, such as the Western Australia gold rush town of Kalgoorlie, made their main streets especially wide to accommodate the turning radius of these long strings of vital pack animals. Camels were used for virtually everything: Hauling ore from remote mines; taking wool clips to market; carrying the mail; and transporting men and equipment during the construction of the Overland Telegraph, the railroad to Alice Springs, and the trans-Australian railroad across the Nullarbor Plain to Perth.

Vital though camels were to opening up their vast arid country, rank-and-file Australians never warmed to them as they did to horses. Camels were regarded as dirty, ill-tempered, and dangerous. They spat, they stank at both ends, and they seemed to take delight in causing mischief. Harry, a cantankerous camel with John Horrocks' 1846 expedition into the South Australian outback, savagely bit expedition members, chased the other animals, and chewed holes in precious bags of flour. Relations between camel and human were eventually strained to the breaking point when Harry shot to death the expedition leader. Horrocks had been loading a rifle when Harry lurched, caught one of his traces around the weapon's cocking mechanism, and discharged it into Horrocks' face. Harry was shot, but not before he'd bitten another stockman.

The skilled camel drivers from Afghanistan and India's North-West Frontier, who had been brought to Australia to handle the beasts, were similarly misunderstood. Mysterious, silent, dark, and turbaned, they were regarded with suspicion by the British community and were forced to live in separate camps and squalid shanties. Known as ghantowns, these sprang up on the outskirts of far-flung settlements such as Bourke, Oodnadatta, Broken Hill, Port Hedland, and Cloncurry. Among the other jobs the cameleers undertook was carrying supplies and building materials to the isolated construction camps of the men building the outback railways.

By the 1930s these railways had made camel trains obsolete. The once-valuable pack animals were simply turned loose in the bush, where their descendants run wild today. There are an estimated 100,000 feral camels in Australia, which is the last country to have herds of the animals. Each year many are captured and exported to the Middle East, or are tamed and used for tourist rides in exotic outback towns such as Broome.

As for the Afghan cameleers, they, too, dispersed. Some returned to the subcontinent; others took jobs on lonely railway maintenance gangs or found their way into the cities, where they blended into Australia's increasingly polyglot population. Today, little more than lonely Muslim grave sites, abandoned mosques, groves of date palms planted in out-of-the-way oases, and the name of the famous train remain to remind outback travelers of this exotic chapter of Australian history.

The episode that inspired the importation of camels to Australia is still remembered throughout the country. More than 10,000 well-wishers lined the streets of Melbourne on August, 20, 1860, to watch Robert O'Hara Burke and William John Wills lead 17 other men and a cavalcade of camels, horses, and wagons northward on a grand adventure to cross the continent. A brass band played, people cheered, and children and dogs ran alongside the parade. It was colonial Australia's equivalent of a moon shot. Lavishly funded by the Victorian government, the expedition's brief was to see "if there really existed in their great continent a Sahara…great lakes…or watered plains which might tempt men to build new cities."

The leader of the expedition, 40-year-old Robert O'Hara Burke was a hot-tempered Irishman and former cavalry officer who had been working as a policeman in rural Victoria. Wills was a starry-eyed 26-year-old surveyor. The expedition carried more than 21 tons of supplies and camp furniture, including an oak table and a dozen beds—and 60 gallons of rum for their camels! The camels themselves had been imported especially for the expedition; the start of the long and proud tradition of using dromedaries and Afghan camel drivers in opening up the outback. Astonishingly, though, given the importance the Victorian government put on the expedition's success, neither Burke nor Wills nor anyone else on the team had had any previous exploration experience or knew much about the Australian outback. By the time the carnival-like procession had reached the outskirts of Melbourne, it was already in trouble. Heavy rains bogged the overburdened wagons. Ahead lay almost 1,400 miles of the hottest, driest, harshest, and loneliest landscape on the planet.

Over the next few weeks the men traveled slowly through the rolling plains, goldfields, and tough mallee scrub of northern Victoria, bickering with each other along the way and pausing periodically to ditch excess gear. Mallee is a gnarled and stunted variety of eucalypt that grows in dense clumps on loose, sandy soils. Horses, camels, and men all found it tough going. At the outback settlement at Menindee, on the lower Darling River, the group divided.

Menindee was a well-known jumping-off place for the outback: Major Thomas Mitchell and Charles Sturt had both camped here during their expeditions in 1835 and 1844. The Menindee hotel—which is still standing today—was regarded as a sort of rough-and-tumble explorers' club. It was here Burke learned that South Australian explorer John Mac-Douall Stuart was about to depart from Adelaide on his third attempt to cross the continent. Suddenly Burke saw his own expedition as a race against that of the tough and vastly more experienced Stuart.

By this time summer was nigh. Ignoring locals' advice that the hot season was a risky time for tenderfeet to head into the desert, Burke set off briskly for Cooper Creek, an isolated string of water holes more than 400 miles away. The plan was to establish a base camp there, from which he and a handpicked team could make a quick push over the final 700 miles to reach the Gulf of Carpentaria. They arrived at Cooper Creek in mid-November—in 110 degree heat.

After waiting a month at Cooper Creek for the slow-moving wagons to catch up, Burke grew impatient. He decided to split his party. Four men would remain at the water hole while Burke, Wills, and two others—Charlie Gray and John King—would make the final push for the gulf. They set off in mid-December—high summer in the outback, when water holes shrink and disappear and a brassy sun flares overhead, bleaching out colors and warping the horizons in shimmering waves of heat.

Several times local Aborigines approached Burke and his men and might have given them invaluable advice, but the neophyte explorers weren't interested. "A large tribe of blacks came pestering us to go to their camp and have a dance, which we declined" wrote Wills in his diary. "They were very troublesome and nothing but the threat to shoot them will keep them away. They are, however, easily frightened and, although fine looking men, decidedly not of a war-like disposition…from the little we have seen of them they appear to be mean spirited and contemptible in every respect." He was to eat those words several brutal months later; unfortunately, by then, they were all he had to eat.

Much of the time the four men traveled by moonlight to escape the searing daytime temperatures. They crossed the Sturt Stony Desert, an apocalyptic landscape of bare, pebbly earth and, farther north, trudged across vast plains dotted with clumps of prickly spinifex.

Over the years spinifex has proved the bane of many outback travelers, myself included. Its sharp, quill-like needles are easily able to penetrate trouser legs, chafing and irritating flesh. As the party traveled farther north, the climate grew hotter and muggier. The monsoon season was imminent. A few miles short of the Gulf of Carpentaria the team's camels became too bogged in the mud to continue.

Burke left King and Gray with the camels while he and Wills pushed on, reaching their farthest point north on February 11, 1861. Impenetrable, crocodile-infested mangrove swamps prevented them from getting a clear view of the ocean, but the taste of saltwater in the creeks told Burke and Wills that they had effectively reached their goal. They rejoined King and Gray and began the long, slow, dreary trudge back to their base camp at Cooper Creek, more than 700 miles away. They were exhausted, provisions were running low, and the heat and humidity never let up. On April 17, just a few days away from base camp, Charlie Gray dropped dead of exhaustion and malnutrition.

Meanwhile, back at Cooper Creek, the rest of the party had given up waiting. Before he left, Burke had said he and his men would be back in three months or less. By now nearly four months had passed, in heat and flies and dust and idleness, without any word of the party. Supplies were running low, and on the morning of April 21 the men pulled out of Cooper Creek and headed south. Before they left, they buried some food and a message in a bottle in case Burke should still be alive and make it to Cooper Creek. They carved instructions—DIG 3FT N.W. APR. 21 1861—onto the bark of a giant coolabah tree that had shaded the camp—and left.

A fateful nine-and-a-half hours later Burke, Wills, and King staggered up to Cooper Creek—and found their camp deserted and the message that the party had left only that morning. "Our disappointment at finding the depot deserted may be easily imagined," wrote Wills, "returning in an exhausted state, after four months of the severest travelling and privation, our legs almost paralyzed so that each of us found it a most trying task only to walk a few yards."

Deciding that they could not possibly overtake the retreating party, the men dug up the provisions left for them, ate, rested overnight, and then set off for the outback police depot at aptly named Mount Hopeless, in South Australia. Before they left, they reburied some provisions, carefully but foolishly erasing their tracks from around the big coolabah tree.

Foolishly, because fate had more tricks to play on the hapless explorers. While they headed off to Mount Hopeless, apparently unaware that there was no water en route, their colleagues had had a change of heart and returned to Cooper Creek for one final check. Seeing the site apparently undisturbed, they left again—this time for good. Ironically, Burke, Wills and King were less than 30 miles away and on their way back, having given up the attempt to reach Mount Hopeless. Too weak to attempt to follow their colleagues, they now had to throw themselves on the good graces of the Aborigines.

Considering the earlier attitudes of the explorers, the Aborigines were remarkably charitable and forgiving, giving the starving white men cakes made from seedlike parts of nardoo, a local drought-resistant fern. But the Aborigines had their own business to attend to and were often gone for days at a time. The explorers tried to make their own nardoo bread, but they lacked the Aborigines'

thousands of years of experience and failed to prepare the mix properly. What they didn't know was that there is an enzyme in the nardoo that robs the body of vitamin B and prevents digestion. The Aborigines' skillful preparation removed these enzymes. The explorers didn't, and they gradually starved on full stomachs.

"I am weaker than ever," Wills wrote in his final journal entry, dated June 29, 1861, "although I have a good appetite and relish the nardoo much; but it seems to give us no nutriment.... Nothing now but the greatest good luck can save any of us; and as for myself I may live four or five days if the weather continues warm. My pulse is at forty-eight, and very weak, and my legs and arms are nearly skin and bone. I can only look out, like Mr. Micawber, 'for something to turn up'." Nothing did. Burke and Wills both perished. Twenty-year-old John King might have followed them into the grave but for the intervention of kindly Aborigines who, "seemed to look upon me as one of themselves, and supplied me with fish and nardoo regularly."

Meanwhile, Burke and Will's redoubtable South Australian rival, John MacDouall Stuart, had met with defeat on his latest attempt to cross the continent. He arrived back in Adelaide in time to hear of Burke and Wills lonely deaths. Neither that somber news nor his own broken health deterred him in the least. Three weeks later he volunteered to lead another expedition. The South Australian government backed him, and on October 25, 1861, he and his men set off on a final attempt to cross the continent.

They reached the sea on July 24 the following year and returned triumphantly to Adelaide in December, without the loss of a single member of the group. Ironically Stuart arrived in the city, a broken but successful explorer, on the very day the bodies of Burke and Wills passed through Adelaide on the way to Melbourne and Victoria's first state funeral.

While the inland explorers and their camel trains were gone for months at a time out over the shimmering horizons, the settlers, prospectors, and graziers they left behind were busily staking out claims and opening up vast tracts of land to sheep, cattle, and the plow. In this, the Burke and Wills expedition achieved an ironic success in its goal of opening up new grazing land. Although the neophyte explorers did not discover much, search parties sent to find them, led by experienced bushmen did. Australia's landed gentry was not far behind. Within a few short years, these wealthy squatters had snapped up much of the best grazing land, laying the foundations for some of Australia's great pastoral dynasties. And while the squatters built their fortunes and elegant homesteads, the rank-and-file Australians began taking imaginative possession of their new country.

The lyrical outback myth was born; its heroes were the rugged, bronzed footloose Aussie swagmen who knocked about the countryside, were always loyal to their mates, and who liked a drink or three at the pub or a bet on the horses. They were proud, good-hearted, immensely competent, none too well fixed for cash, had a laconic sense of humor, and generally lived a better, freer life than their confined city cousins. The *Bulletin* magazine, launched in Sydney in 1880, helped establish these romantic images of the Australian bush, showcasing poems and folksy vignettes of bush life by the likes of Andrew Barton "Banjo" Paterson and his dour and down-at-the-heels contemporary, Henry Lawson.

There was certainly no shortage of material or colorful characters. One such bloke was Henry Redford, a stockman who drifted around the sprawling cattle stations in the dusty central Queensland outback in 1870. Redford was a skilled bushman who had taken the trouble to learn the rhythms of the land from the Aborigines and how to find food and water. Redford spoke several of their languages. Equipped with these formidable talents, he and his gang spirited away a thousand cattle from the giant Bowen Downs Station. Their getaway was one of the great cattle drives of all time: More than a thousand miles through the same harsh, arid, little known country that had killed Burke and Wills only decades earlier. The rustlers moved the herd all the way to Adelaide, where they sold the cattle for £5,000.

They might have got away with it, except that a conspicuous white shorthorn bull—imported from England for stud duties—had tagged along behind them like a faithful puppy. Its distinctive appearance ultimately betrayed them. Later Redford was arrested and hauled back to Roma, Queensland, for trial—the white shorthorn bull accompanied him as a witness for the prosecution—

but his daring cattle drive had so fired the public's imagination that no jury of his outback peers would convict him. Rural Queenslanders—who love to tell this story—have it that the jury returned a quixotic verdict of: "Not guilty, but he's got to give the cattle back!" And when the outraged magistrate ordered them to reconsider, they did—this time supposedly returning with an ornery: "Not guilty, and he can keep the bloody cattle!"

The Brisbane *Courier* reported that "they have a curious practice in the far west of this colony of pulling fellows for cattle stealing and taking them to Roma to be tried by a jury of their peers, who enjoy the fun amazingly and after going through a form of evidence and making a few bovine jokes, bring in a verdict of 'Not Guilty'." After Redford's remarkable acquittal, the court at Roma lost its jurisdiction to hear cattle rustling cases for two years.

While Redford went on to more adventures—and further rustling charges—in the tropical north, his old stomping ground in central Queensland went on to midwife some of Australia's most enduring and defining legends. They were men like Big Jackie Howe, Australia's real-life answer to Paul Bunyan and steel-driving John Henry, a champion shearer who lived near Blackall.

Born in 1861, Howe was the son of a circus acrobat. A strapping young athlete in his own right, he learned the skills for which he was to become so famous from Chinese shearers. Shearing sheds are intensely competitive places, with an emphasis on speed and endurance, and Howe quickly established a reputation as Australia's greatest shearer, regularly notching up tallies of 250 sheep in a day. At Alice Downs station in October 1892, Howe chalked up his greatest ever tally: 321 lambs in a union-prescribed day of 7 hours and 40 minutes.

It is a record that has never been beaten, at least not by anyone using the kind of old-fashioned hand-powered shears Howe used. (And it was 1942 before anyone topped it using electric shears.) Howe left behind another legacy that went well beyond the shearing shed: The style of sleeveless navy blue singlet his wife made for him, to give him ease of movement, was adopted by working class Australians everywhere and is known to this day as a Jackie Howe.

More outback legends were forged 60 miles farther north, in the town of Barcaldine, which became the strike headquarters for more than a thousand shearers during a bitter strike in 1891. Their fiery gatherings beneath the limbs of a 200-year-old gum tree, still standing and known as the "tree of knowledge," provided the catalyst for the founding of the Australian Labor Party the following year.

About a 170 miles northwest of Barcaldine is the town of Winton, the birthplace in 1920 of another Aussie emblem, the Queensland & Northern Territory Aerial Service, the airline known today the world over by its acronym: Qantas. Perhaps the most stirring bit of Aussie folklore came out of Winton. It is where Banjo Paterson reputedly wrote the lyrics to "Waltzing Matilda," Australia's unofficial national anthem.

One story has it that Paterson wrote "Waltzing Matilda" while visiting a lady friend named Christina Macpherson at nearby Dagworth Station in 1895. The exact history behind the song and the tune has been lost over the decades in claim, counterclaim, wishful thinking, and myth. The lyrics, which are so freighted with outback slang that they are almost incomprehensible to non-Australians, tell the story of a happy-go-lucky vagabond who, while camped beneath a coolabah tree, butchers a stolen sheep for his dinner. As he is cooking it, three mounted troopers ride up. Rather than be arrested and lose his cherished freedom, the hobo dives into a nearby pond and defiantly drowns himself.

A century later the song still tugs on Australian imaginations. Some listeners believe "Waltzing Matilda" has its roots in the pro-labor politics of the day, a sympathetic note for the defiant striking shearers who were to help form the Australian Labor Party. Others believe it was simply a folksy local story put to rhyme by Paterson in order to please his hostess, who in turn put it to an old English military tune. Some believe the source of the melody is an old Scottish ballad. Whatever its origins, within a very few years after Paterson wrote it, the evocative "Waltzing Matilda" became—and remains—Australia's best loved tune.

There is more to the outback myth than lean and lanky riders, roving crews of shearers, and ne'er-do-well swagmen. Some of the world biggest mineral deposits have been found in the Precambrian rocks of Australia's outback, and they've inspired some of the most colorful towns in the outback: Mount Isa, Broken Hill, Kalgoorlie, and the rollicking opal fields of Coober Pedy, in the remote South Australian outback.

Coober Pedy—a corruption of an Aboriginal phrase *kupa piti*, or white man in a hole—was discovered by chance by a teenage boy in 1915, and over the past 80 years a unique community of hardened adventurers, drifters, and fortune hunters from 45 nations has sprung up around it.

The first time I drove into the town along the desolate Stuart Highway, I had a feeling I was approaching a set from one of the apocalyptic *Mad Max* movies. Indeed, much of *Mad Max III* was shot here. For miles around the landscape is dotted with eerie conical piles of rubble from the more than 250,000 holes made by opal miners. They look somehow evil in fading desert twilight. People here live underground: Many of its residents live in caves to escape the burning heat of summer. These cave homes, hotels, and businesses are surprisingly pleasant and airy, and their well-insulated rooms remain a constant and comfortable 72 degrees. Home expansion is a simple matter of digging out a new room in the dense clay, with perhaps the occasional opal find to help defray your costs. That is one of the joys of Coober Pedy: Anyone with a prospecting permit has an equal chance of striking it rich. Opals are randomly distributed throughout the rich red earth. One hole has as good a chance as another at striking a band of fiery black opal, the most valuable type, which can be worth tens of thousands of dollars.

Perhaps Australia's most colorful mining town is Broken Hill, New South Wales, near the South Australia border. In 1883 Charles Rasp, a German-born drover on a remote sheep station, stumbled onto an enormous mineral-rich formation with the aid of a how-to-prospect guidebook he'd purchased while on holiday in Adelaide.

it out, found some backers, and went into mining. Later the investors realized they had found a mountain of galena-sphalerite ore, almost unimaginably rich in silver, lead, and zinc. At 280 million tons, the six-mile-long, boomerang-shaped ore body remains to this day the biggest and richest of its type ever found.

Rasp and his partners became incredibly rich, and their company, Broken Hill Proprietary (BHP), became Australia's largest corporation. Several more of Australia's great mining houses—such as CRA and North Limited—also sprang from these metal-rich rocks about 570 miles west of Sydney.

By the early years of the century, Broken Hill had a rowdy population of more than 30,000 and supported more than a hundred hotels and pubs. It was known throughout the world for its quick wealth, wild living, and the increasingly bitter conflicts between labor and management. The town of Broken Hill became a honey pot for prospectors, adventurers, radical American unionists who had been chased out of Chicago, strong-backed miners, and company men. A mining engineer named Herbert Hoover, who later became President of the United States, was another visitor who passed through "the Hill."

Vast wealth and the mines' enormous staying power created an architecturally rich town. Argent Street, the city's main thoroughfare, is crammed with elegant Victorian two- and three-story pubs, their balconies embellished with traceries of ornamental iron lace. Broken Hill's town hall is opulently Italianate, the trades-hall building is an effusive mix of baroque styles, while the headquarters of the North Broken Hill Mine is a stunning piece of art deco.

More than a century after Rasp discovered it, the Broken Hill orebody continues to produce enormous wealth. It is now waning, however, and by 2006 mining is expected to cease. Today, the "silver city" is looking to the silver screen for jobs. Broken Hill's 300-plus days of sunshine, clear desert air, and its regular air links with Sydney have made it a hot location for filmmakers and the advertising industry. Set designers, casting agencies, and location scouts have set up businesses here, and bemused locals often get work as extras.

Movies such as *Mad Max II* and *Priscilla, Queen of the Desert* were filmed here. Coca-Cola's famous sky-surfing commercial was shot over the Mundi Mundi plains, an hour's drive north of Broken Hill. Levi's, Pepsi, Toyota, and XXXX Beer have all filmed high-profile commercials in and around Broken Hill, and rock groups such as INXS have shot video clips here. The ghost town of Silverton, about 15 miles north of Broken Hill, is an especially popular filming venue. Its colorful pub, the Silverton Hotel, has been renamed more than a dozen times for its film, commercial, and TV mini-series appearances.

The same fragile desert light and dramatic outback scenery that attract the film industry have also brought some of Australia's best artists to Broken Hill. Known as the "brushmen of the bush," the group includes such nationally prominent names as Pro Hart and Jack Absalom. The once rough mining town is now dotted with art galleries and bright with murals. And on a hilltop on the northern outskirts of town are 12 sandstone sculptures. Created by sculptors from around Australia and overseas, they exude a kind of Stonehenge quality in the ancient landscape.

I went out there one evening around sundown, walking among the haunting statues. I looked out across the desert and the delicate mauves and pinks in the western sky. Early lights twinkled in Broken Hill. Far off in the distance I watched the high beams of a truck booming along the Barrier Highway bound for a distant Sydney.

Following pages: *Sunlight shimmers on the ancient, wind-scoured rocks of the Balgo Hills in Western Australia's Great Sandy Desert. Recent rains have freshened the trees and grasses huddled in the normally dry watercourses.*

Haunting lunette sand dunes of Mungo National Park, in western New South Wales, conceal an almost unbroken record of more than 60,000 years of Aboriginal history. Among the discoveries: The remains of the world's earliest known cremation were unearthed here, a simple ceremony that took place about 26,000 years ago on the shore of what was then a chain of freshwater lakes.

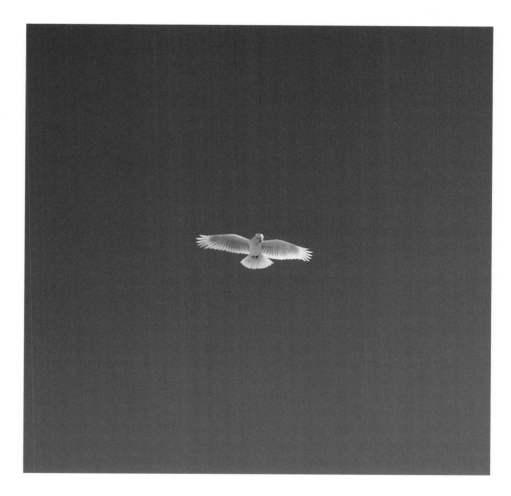

Early morning sun catches the brilliantly hued wings of a pink cockatoo as it soars into blue skies over Lake Mungo. These raucous birds—known colloquially as desert cockatoos—flit around the outback in flocks of 30 or more, often erupting from the bush in a rush of noise and color.

Following pages: *A lonely cattle station known as Old Andado appears lost in the timeless waves of sand dunes that cover the vast Simpson Desert. This hostile void defied early explorers' attempts to cross it, and it was not until 1929, when aerial surveys began, that the thousand parallel dunes of the Simpson Desert were finally mapped. Rains can transform the seemingly lifeless desert into waving grasslands almost overnight.*

Rising eerily from the flat plains in Australia's red center, the 600 million-year-old sandstone monolith known as Uluru casts a hypnotic spell that has drawn travelers toward it for thousands of years. Once known only to the Anangu Aborigines, it is now one of Australia's most universally recognized symbols. Perhaps a quarter-of-a-million visitors make the pilgrimage here each year.

Out for an evening joyride, a group of Aborigines bounce along a dusty track near the community of Balgo, on the eastern fringe of Western Australia's Great Sandy Desert. Open-air excursions in the back of a truck are both social events and a popular way to defeat the desert's heat at the end of the day.

An Aboriginal family unwinds in front of a television in the warmth of a desert evening at the Balgo community in remote Western Australia. Although the government provides housing, many Aborigines prefer the traditional open-air lifestyles of their ancestors, sleeping and eating in their yards until winter arrives.

Desperate and determined, a wild horse lands headfirst after leaping a gate to escape a stockman's rope at Innaminka Station. The ranch, spread along Cooper Creek in the northeastern corner of Queensland, covers 5,500 square miles.

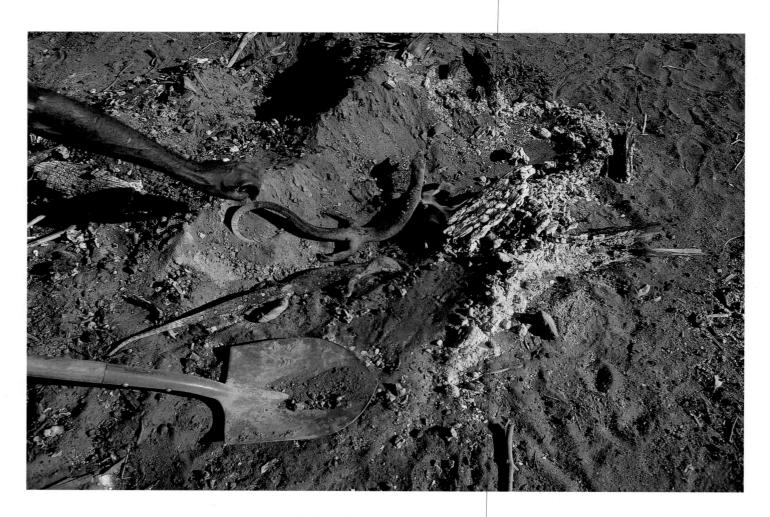

Cooked in the coals of a dying camp-fire, goanna—a sand monitor lizard—is a prized delicacy in Yagga Yagga, a remote Aboriginal community near the Great Sandy Desert. The Aborigines of Yagga Yagga have broken away from social problems in other communities and have returned to the traditional lifestyle of their ancestors.

Aboriginal hunter Mark Moora returns victorious from the bush with his kill—a wild turkey. Although the last of the purely nomadic Aborigines quit the desert in 1984 in favor of a more Western style of life in communities, a growing number of Aborigines, such as Moora, are returning at least part-time to some of the old traditions.

Following pages: *Guided by the domes of Kata Tjuta, Robyn Davidson leads her camel train westward across broad spinifex plains in central Australia. Davidson made an epic camel trek across the outback in 1977. Until the early 1930s camels carried freight in the outback. Today, their descendants run wild in the bush.*

Sly predator: A dingo slinks away from a water hole. Believed to have been brought to Australia from Southeast Asia by seafarers about 3,500 years ago, these slightly built feral dogs hunt kangaroos, rodents, and lizards. For the past two centuries, however, their easiest pickings have been slow-moving sheep, setting the stage for a ceaseless war between humans and dingoes.

Bounding the world's biggest back-yard, the Dog Fence stretches 3,307 miles through the outback from Queensland to the west coast of South Australia. Conceived in 1880 to protect sheep from dingoes, the fence requires vigilant patrolling and constant maintenance. Dingoes inside the fence are classed as vermin and can be shot on sight. Bounties for dingoes run as high $500.

Sudden rock slides can crush vehicles working in the pit of a gold mine; fortunately no one was injured in the accident at the giant Telfer Mine, in Western Australia, that crumpled this cab. Although vastly safer than it was in the old days, mining remains one of Australia's riskier occupations. Nevertheless, fat pay checks and the prospect of adventure lure thousands of Australians into the outback each year.

King of outback highways, a double-decker road train hauls about 200 cattle to the Mareeba saleyards from Dunbar Station in the Cape York Peninsula. These massive triple-trailer rigs can weigh as much as 140 tons and be half as long as a football field. As they thunder along the remote desert tracks they throw up gravel and clouds of talc-fine bull dust.

Following pages: *In a swirl of dust a pack of snarling Australian cattle dogs musters a shorthorn bullock into a drafting pen on Sandringham Station in Queensland's Simpson Desert. Once this scene would have been preceded by a several-month-long cattle drive through the out-back. Now massive road trains haul beef to market in a day or so.*

Rodeos, stock trials, and horse races, such as this one in the outback South Australian town of Marla, draw crowds from stations hundreds of miles away. A rough-hewn cama-raderie prevails at these events, with range gossip, shouted beers, the occasional punch, and thousands of dollars in wagers exchanging hands.

Bruised but unconquered, champion rider Richard Nunn (above, at right), head stockman for the giant Anna Creek Station, rests beneath laurels won at a stock trial in nearby Marla. Although road trains have replaced old-time cattle drives, horses still play a role in roundups on the big stations.

Tank-topped local hero throws a haymaker at a member of Fred Brophy's Boxing Troupe, which visited town for the races in Birdsville, Queensland. Traveling boxing shows, in which locals test their mettle against a pro, have long been a feature of outback entertainment. In this case the 30-dollar purse went to the challenger.

The Birdsville Races, held the first weekend in September, are one of the high points of the outback social calendar. Almost overnight the population of the remote community swells from 80 to more than 6,000, and so many light aircraft empty skies that the Civil Aviation Safety Authority has had to impose special race weekend flight regulations to control traffic on the town's landing strip.

Following pages: *Irrigation from the Murray-Darling River system has transformed the harsh outback scrub of Queensland's Darling Downs into vast—and lucrative—cotton fields. Bales await tarpaulins and shipment to distant city markets.*

Monuments to ambition: 250,000 entrances to mine shafts dot the landscape around the opal-mining town of Coober Pedy, in South Australia's arid outback. Since opals were discovered in 1915, thousands of fortune hunters have flocked here, pick in hand, to try their luck. The law allows each prospector a 165-foot-square claim, effectively shutting out big mining companies.

Like most residents of the opal mining community of White Cliffs, in outback New South Wales, 80-year-old prospector and artist Ivy Kennedy lives underground to escape savage 115-degree heat on the surface. Insulated by the chalky earth, her home stays at 72 degrees year-round. An illuminated aquarium takes the place of a wished-for skylight.

Evening rush hour is light on the main street of Rutherglen, a farming village in the cool highlands of northern Victoria. The scene of a rollicking gold rush in 1862, the historic town is now known for its century-old vineyards and fine wines.

Following pages: *Clear skies above White Cliffs have a silver lining. With an average of more than 300 sun-drenched days a year, the town was a natural site for the world's first experimental solar power station. Built in 1981, the array of 14 dishes, each a little more than 16 feet in diameter, generates a total of about 42 kilowatts of electricity an hour and is monitored by a video link to a control center in Melbourne.*

At various times of the year Ningaloo Reef becomes the playground of dugongs, sea turtles, dolphins, humpback whales, and whale sharks. World's largest fish, these gentle plankton-eating giants congregate in these waters in the autumn, drawing divers from all over the world.

Shark Bay, on the World Heritage list, is another powerful tourist drawing card. As the name suggests, the bay teems with marine life thanks to thick sea grass beds that provide food and shelter to huge schools of fish, dugongs, and sea snakes. But it is for its gregarious dolphin population that Shark Bay is most famous. For more than 30 years dolphins have swum into the shallows near the town of Monkey Mia to play with humans, accept fish from them, and offer them gifts of fish.

For many years it was simply a game between marine biologists and the dolphins, but by 1985, when the road to Monkey Mia was finally paved, easy access and a rare opportunity to interact with wild dolphins brought thousands of tourists. Shark Bay also has 70-mile-long Shell Beach, one of the few beaches in the world that is made entirely of non-fossilized shells: billions upon billions of tiny coquina bivalves in beds up to 40 feet thick.

A hundred miles farther south, Kalbarri National Park's spectacular sandstone gorges and the Murchison River are among Western Australia's most popular parks, particularly in the spring. Then the wildflowers come into bloom, and the park becomes a kaleidoscope of grevilleas, banksias, melaleucas, leschenaultias, and sedges.

Stories of the Conte de Saint-Allouarn's claiming this region for France—by now only a matter of historical curiosity—had been circulating since a historian had come across a reference to it in some musty 18th-century archives in Paris after World War I. There was never any proof of the claim, and in fact some of the Conte de Saint-Allouarn's contemporaries in Paris doubted that he'd even set foot in Australia. But in December 1997 archaeologists digging on a hilltop on Dirk Hartog Island made an intriguing find: Two silver French coins, dating from the early 1770s, and a weathered 18th-century wine bottle.

Whatever the Conte de Saint-Allouarn did or didn't do on Dirk Hartog Island, French navigators continued to explore the coast. Aware that the French might establish a base in Western Australia, in 1826 the governor of New South Wales set up a penal colony on King George Sound, where the town of Albany is today. The flag was raised, and the new settlement was christened Frederick's Town, after the Duke of York and Albany. The pleasant seaport on the cool, breezy southwest corner of the continent quickly became a regular port of call for French and American whalers and is known today for its fishing fleet.

English authorities were still nervous about French intentions, however, and when an ambitious English Navy post captain named James Stirling approached them with the idealistic notion of starting a colony of free settlers along the Swan River, they accepted the idea. Nobody knew if the settlement would be viable or not. At the colonial office nobody really cared so long as a new English presence was going to be established on the coast, particularly since private investors were footing the bill. The eager colonists went off, in the words of one contemporary, "without any greater preparation than if they had gone out on a holiday excursion in the woods." In the autumn of 1829, they landed on the coast in a torrential rain and established the town of Fremantle, where the Swan River meets the sea. A few months later some of the party relocated about nine miles upstream, and on August 12, 1829, they proclaimed the town of Perth.

After grandiose speeches and musketry salutes, the pilgrims were left to confront a few harsh realities: They were surrounded by marshland humming with mosquitoes and sand fleas, as far from civilization as any place could be, and nobody else wanted to join them. Why migrate here when, if you wanted to go to the colonies, you could always go to New South Wales? Sydney was a prosperous young city, land was freely available and, better still, free convict labor was available to work it. Consequently Perth attracted few migrants.

For the next 20 years it languished, a dismal shanty-town, until in 1850 its leaders relented and began to import convicts to do the grunt work of building public edifices, bridges, and roads. At last Perth began to take shape, and in 1856 it was proclaimed a city. Even so, remoteness and lack of interest made Perth the poor relation to the rest of Australia until 1887. Then a boy near Halls Creek, in the remote Kimberley region on the northwest frontier, picked up a stone to fling at a crow and noticed it was laced with gold. Word of the find spread like wildfire, triggering the first of a fantastic sequence of gold, silver, tin, copper, and manganese strikes. Western Australia has hardly looked back.

Perth today is a sun-splashed city of a million with a glittering skyline along the Swan River, a new-money brashness, and a reputation for being Australia's answer to Dallas. Most of the big money here comes from the west's vast mineral wealth—iron, oil, gold, natural gas, and diamonds—and, like Texas, Perth carries itself with a big-hatted frontier swagger. Back in the rollicking 1980s, it was home to Australia's highest-flying corporate buccaneers, a clique of ruthless, fabulously wealthy self-made entrepreneurs. The nouveau riche excesses—gleaming yachts, private jets, and priceless French impressionists on boardroom walls—of these Gatsbyesque figures defined a jazzy new era for the rest of Australia.

No one personified it better than Alan Bond. A sign-painter turned millionaire property developer and swashbuckling yachtsman, Bond tweaked the old-money noses of the New York Yacht Club in 1983 and took the America's Cup back to Australia in a stunning upset that made him a national hero. But Bond was only one of a coterie of Perth businessmen who became household names and whose faces shone from glossy celebrity magazines. As the decade of junk bonds and conspicuous consumption took shape, the Golden West took on the glow of a magic strike-it-rich place where anything could happen—and frequently did.

Like the gold rush prospectors, pearling masters, and Afghan cameleers who shaped so much of Western Australia's frontier myths, Perth's high-rolling entrepreneurs have largely passed into oblivion—or minimum security prisons. The music stopped after the October 1987 world stock market crash, when public adulation was replaced by the harder scrutiny of a royal commission, police investigations, and deliberating juries. Details of insider deals, art fraud, rigged horse races, and millions of dollars vanishing in the snap of bejeweled fingers alternately fascinated, amused, and outraged the rest of Australia. It still tends to view Western Australia as a world apart.

Even in these days of jet travel and instant communications, Western Australia is seriously remote. Perth is often said to be the loneliest city in the world. Its nearest similar-size neighbor, Adelaide, is 1,300 air miles away, and to get there you have to cross the vast treeless, water-

less void known as the Nullarbor Plain. The flight from Sydney takes five hours and, until the airlines started using long-haul Boeing 767s, westbound planes battling head winds often had to make unscheduled fuel stops in Adelaide before tackling the Nullarbor. But it is traveling overland that really brings home the immense distance between Perth and the rest of the world.

Every Monday and Thursday at 2:55 p.m. the *Indian Pacific* pulls out of Sydney's grand, domed Central Railway Station to begin one of the world's great train journeys: across the Australian outback 2,703 miles to Perth. The trip takes 65 hours and crosses some of the most barren and lifeless landscapes on the planet, where temperatures often soar to 120 degrees. One stretch of track, laid across the waterless heart of the Nullarbor Plain, is billed as the world's longest straightaway—310 miles of dead straight rail from a lonely siding called Ooldea, where a few railway maintenance workers live, to a slight bend at another siding called Nurina.

The origin of this trans-Australian rail link goes back to the late 19th century. It was offered as an inducement for the reluctant Western Australia to join the other colonies in forming a united Australian nation. Construction started from the South Australian town of Port Augusta in 1914. While there were no major engineering obstacles to laying a thousand miles of track across the Nullarbor Plain, the project was a logistical nightmare, the Edwardian era's version of building a space station. Since there was nothing in this void to sustain life, everything—food, water, shelter for thousands of workers and pack animals—had to be hauled out into the desert. Portable communities were set up, their butchers, bakers, banks, and post offices on rolling stock ready to be shifted farther along newly laid line as the track stretched deeper into the hostile wastes. Fresh provisions were sent out from Port Augusta every two weeks.

For some 60 years these isolated communities were serviced by the legendary Tea and Sugar Train, a weekly supply line from Port Augusta that brought everything from fresh water to Santa Claus. Airplanes now supply the few remaining settlements.

After the long journey across the continent, Perth appears on the horizon like the Emerald City of Oz. The sudden surge of wealth from Western Australia's huge iron, diamond, and natural gas discoveries in the 1960s and 1970s almost completely transformed the city center. Gone are old buildings, replaced by modern glass-and-steel office towers and sunlit shopping precincts that give the city a fresh youthfulness not found even in other Australian cities, young as they are by world standards. Perth suburbs are a sprawl of 1950s-style Californian bungalows, their swimming pools, television aerials, palms, and jacaranda trees all projecting the same sunny, egalitarian optimism.

Nine miles southwest, where the Swan River meets the Indian Ocean, is the historic seaport of Fremantle, one of the world's best preserved 19th-century maritime cities. Once a working-class domain of Italian fishermen and Irish longshoremen, its fading colonial facades taste-fully smartened up for Australia's unsuccessful defense of the America's Cup yachting trophy in 1987, Fremantle remains a raffishly fashionable enclave for Perth's arty set, café society, and professionals escaping both the city and the suburbs. Although it is very close to Perth, Fremantle has strongly retained its distinct identity. About a dozen miles beyond its dazzling white beach, a short ferry ride away, is Rottnest Island—one of Perth's traditional play-grounds for divers, sailors, and beach-lovers.

Fremantle is a sports-mad city that rejoices in its hot dry Mediterranean climate. On weekends its beaches are crowded with bronzing Aussies, the Swan River is bright with yachts, and the parks become playing fields for scores of informal cricket or football matches. The subur-ban air is fragrant with the smoke of countless barbecues. Even so, in Perth you never lose the sense of being on the edge of the frontier. The flocks of parrots swooping down the streets, and the possums, small kangaroos, and snakes in the parklands are subtle reminders of the vast expanse of bush that stretches thousands of miles beyond the city.

South of Perth the coast becomes cooler and rainier. A big surf washes the shores, and a hinterland rolls deep in the shade of some of the world's tallest timber—tower-ing karri trees, a type of eucalypt that can reach up to 300 feet high. This is some of the prettiest, greenest country in Western Australia, with narrow country lanes, sparkling beaches, farmlands, and orchards. Over the past 35 years this extreme southwesterly outcrop on the continent has been discovered by successive waves of hippies, surfers, wealthy yuppies looking for weekend retreats, artists,

wine-makers, and urban refugees. They give these farming communities a relaxed, offbeat flavor.

Yallingup, about 125 miles southwest of Perth, has been a honeymoon retreat for wealthy couples since the turn of the century, but it was the surfing boom of the 1960s that put it on the map. The reliably huge waves that pound the sands here have made it the traditional location for the Australia surfing competitions and a mecca for globetrotting, summer-seeking surfers. Breaking waves are a lifestyle and a class leveler along this stretch of coast. Go to any of the surf beaches from Yallingup south to Cape Leeuwin, and in the parking lots you'll see an odd mix of gleaming, late-model BMWs and battered Kombi vans out of the sixties. Their owners are all out in the 15-foot waves.

Some of the finest scenery here is underground, in a labyrinth of limestone caves—more than a hundred in all. Many are relatively unexplored. A few, such as Mammoth Cave, Lake Cave, and Jewel Cave, with its delicate crys-tals, have become major tourist drawing cards.

Back on the surface, the limestone bedrock chal-lenges wine grapes to do their best. More than 40 vine-yards—Leeuwin Estate, Cape Mentelle, and Cullen, among other Australian top labels—are centered around the farming community of Margaret River, which is rapidly gaining a following among connoisseurs.

Cape Leeuwin marks the extreme southwest corner of the continent, where the forces of the Indian Ocean and Southern Ocean meet. The Dutch ship *Leeuwin* (Lioness) was blown here in 1622. Never before had a Dutch ship ventured this far south on the Australian coast. Almost two centuries later, in 1801, Matthew Flinders used the cape as the marker for his circumnavigation of the conti-nent, naming the storm-lashed point of land after the Dutch ship.

Western Australia's southern coast is shrouded by solemn forests of jarrah and karri trees and indented by scores of bays and inlets. The timber town of Pemberton claims the tallest karri tree ever felled in the district, a 338-foot-tall giant. Visitors with a good head for heights can climb up 153 rungs that spiral up the massive trunk of the Gloucester Tree to a viewing platform nearly 200 feet high. Closer to the coast, where rainfall is heaviest, Walpole-Nornalup National Park boasts a magnificent stand of tingle trees known as the Valley of the Giants.

Mingled among them are rich stands of casuarina trees, flowering banksias, wild orchids, and felt-like wildflowers called kangaroo paws.

Each spring much of Western Australia becomes a garden of flowers, more than 12,000 species in all. Most of these are unique to Western Australia. Visitors are drawn here from around the world. From October to December flowers seem to be everywhere—even in downtown Perth as Kings Park riots with color. But no place is more richly or colorfully carpeted than the southwest. Perhaps the most spectacular displays are in the Stirling Range, a ragged chain of mountains about 250 miles southeast of Perth. Some of the exposed summits, which are often shrouded with mist, rise more than 3,000 feet above the surrounding coastal plains. Like lofty islands, surrounded by farmland instead of sea, these slopes support their own unique ecology. There are more than a thousand species of wildflowers up here, some of which, like darwinias, dryandras, and Stirling banksias, are found nowhere else. Beyond these ranges the land flattens out and opens up toward the goldfields, the Nullarbor Plain, and the wild, cliff-lined coast of the Great Australian Bight.

The early string of gold strikes in the Kimberley and Pilbara that helped turn Western Australia's fortunes in the late 1880s were merely flashes in the pan compared with the stunning Coolgardie and Kalgoorlie finds in the 1890s. Gold fever struck in September 1892, when two prospectors, Arthur Bayley and William Ford, rode into the mining town of Southern Cross with almost 35 pounds of gold nuggets they had picked up near a water hole. Thousands stampeded to the area, some on camels. Others walked the final 150 miles across arid plains from the railhead at Southern Cross, sometimes pushing wheelbarrows. Tent cities sprang up. And as more prospectors spread out, scouring the ground, more pulse-quickening discoveries were made nearby—at Norseman, Kambalda, Kanowna, and Kookynie. But it was a lucky Irishman named Paddy Hannan who found the mother of all mother lodes in 1893—an unbelievably rich quartz vein running through Mount Charlotte. Reputedly, Hannan

was chasing an errant horse at the time. A century later his find remains one of the world's richest gold-bearing areas, and Kalgoorlie, the boisterous town that sprang up around it, is synonymous with wealth and opportunity. Since those first heady days, a staggering 1,300 tons of gold have come out of Kalgoorlie's fabled Golden Mile. More than 800,000 ounces—about 25 tons, or 350 million dollars worth of gold—is still produced here each year.

By 1902 more than 30,000 people were living in Kalgoorlie, making it slightly larger than it is today. The town had 93 pubs and 8 breweries, and its railway line was the busiest in the state. To keep the rapidly growing gold town alive on this waterless waste, a 345-mile-long pipeline was built in 1903 to bring in water from a reservoir near Perth.

Kalgoorlie's streetscapes are pure Australian gold rush: An exuberant hodgepodge of Edwardian, Moorish, and Victorian styles done in stone, brick, and corrugated iron, and embellished with verandas, balconies, gables, and towers. The town, which amalgamated with nearby Boulder in 1989, still has a frontier flair. It is famous—or infamous—for its topless barmaids (known as "skimpys"), its hard-drinking macho atmosphere, and its boisterous games of two-up, a uniquely outback Australian gambling game in which punters bet on the toss of two coins. For many Australians the vast West Australia goldfields represent a place of opportunity, whether for high-paying jobs in the mines, or for the outrageous good fortune of the husband and wife prospectors who found a 97-ounce nugget in nearby Coolgardie.

Fittingly, these goldfield settlements are the first towns of any size westbound travelers see after crossing the long empty wastes of the Nullarbor Plain. They set the tone for the Golden West. For people leaving it, heading east on the Eyre Highway out of Norseman, a foreboding sign warns that along this harsh stretch of the southern shore there will be few places to get water for the next 800 miles.

Following pages: *A traveler trails a plume of dust near the abandoned asbestos-mining town of Wittenoom, in Western Australia's Hamersley Range. Health fears forced the closing of the mine in 1966.*

Drifting past a diver, a 35-foot-long whale shark patrols the placid waters of Western Australia's Ningaloo Reef. World's largest fish, whale sharks pose no threat to most reef creatures. The shy fish feed on plankton.

"An upside down snowstorm," divers often say, describing the magical nights in March when corals along Ningaloo Reef release their eggs and sperm. Spawning on the Southern Hemisphere's coral reefs occurs each autumn, usually after the full moon. Carried along by the tides, the fertilized eggs will attach themselves to the skeletal remains of dead corals and begin a new colony.

*Discovered in 1989 and unique to
the shallows of Hamelin Pool, a
species of jellyfish known as* Phyl-
lorhiza peronlesueuri *floats above
a bed of 4,000-year-old stromatolites,
a form of blue-green algae. Tucked
in a recess in Western Australia's
Shark Bay, Hamelin Pool's sheltered,
sunny, and ultra-saline waters make
it ideal sanctuary.*

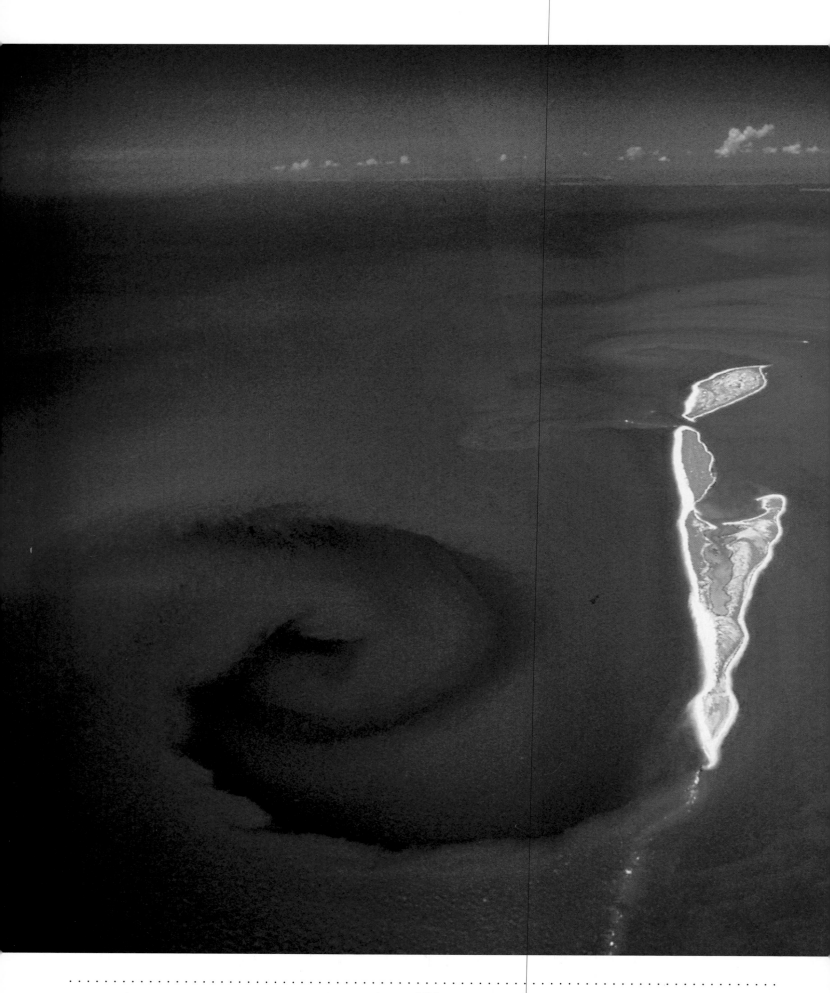

Calm indigo waters, gleaming sands, and a seabed littered with pearl oysters give the Lacepede Islands the look of a paradise, but this lonely archipelago on Western Australia's ragged northwest coast is prey to the capricious winds and treacherous tides of summer monsoons. A tropical cyclone in April 1935 caught the pearling fleet unaware, sinking 21 boats and claiming 140 lives. Divers say copper diving helmets of the dead still roll along the bottom of the sea.

Following pages: Ancient gorges of the Pilbara region plunge into sandstones dating back more than two billion years. Dotted with waterfalls and secluded pools, these deep, palm-lined chasms are havens for birds, kangaroos, and reptiles.

Shaft of sun illuminates a dark pool and sandstone face in Karijini National Park. Eons of runoff from torrential rains have scoured dramatic gorges in the park, part of Western Australia's Pilbara region. Many of the gorges have year-round pools in the dry season.

Hiking into history, tour guide Dave Doust of Wittenoom leads a group on a precipitous walk into a gorge in Karijini National Park. The gorges of the Pilbara, eroded by ancient storms, plummet into bedrock walls that are among the oldest exposed rocks on Earth.

Following pages: Two centuries of shifting dunes have exposed thousands of golden limestone knobs that give the Pinnacles Desert its name. Wind, rain, and sand sculpted the pinnacles, creating an eerie landscape of brooding statues, the main attraction of Nambung National Park.

A brilliant shawl of wildflowers drapes the desert near the mining town of Mount Magnet. Spring rains deck much of Australia's southwest in a dazzling floral display. More than 12,000 species of flowering plants can be found in Western Australia, ranging from giant hardwood trees to tiny underground orchids.

*A flash of pink as a galah takes wing
adds a spark of color to the muted
tones of the bush in Nambung
National Park. Pink-and-gray
galahs, one of the most common of
the 60 species of parrots and cockatoos found in Australia, often flit
along roadsides searching for seeds.*

more efficient at high speeds than the quadrupedal gait of placental animals, but it has some obvious disadvantages at slow speeds. Kangaroos and wallabies use their tail as a prop when standing and as a lever to awkwardly lift their hind legs forward when moving slowly as they graze. The animals cannot move backwards easily.

The bird fauna of Australia is very rich and diverse, with some 700 species compared to 750 in all of North America. Australia has the world's most varied groups of parrots, which include cockatoos, a large number of bright-colored seed-eating parrots, and specialized nectar feeders, the lorikeets. Of all Australian birds the lyrebird is perhaps the most striking and unusual. The male's lyre-shaped plumage, dancing routine, and extraordinary mimicry make the bird stand out. Possessed of a singular song of its own, the male lyrebird intersperses that call with the mimicked songs of numerous birds in its locality. His song, which varies in content of mimicry from place to place, is so intense and clear that it can be heard over long distances in dense scrub and fern gullies.

Other birds unique to Australia and New Guinea include birds of paradise and the bowerbird. The most spectacularly plumaged birds of paradise occur in New Guinea, but representatives of the bowerbird are more evenly distributed. These birds build a bower, which may consist of a platform and an avenue of upright sticks, where courting and mating usually take place. The male adorns his bower with various objects, with scant concern as to their origin, to attract a female. Often the objects are of one color. The satin bowerbird, which favors blue, collects things as diverse as berries, feathers, bits of paper, cloth, and glass.

Scientists once thought that the majority of Australian bird families were related to Asian birds that had migrated to Australia through Indonesia in the distant past. Recent studies using DNA technology, however, suggest that the birds are mostly of ancient Australian stock and have evolved in isolation over long periods. That they resemble Asian birds is a function of adopting similar habits in similar environments.

The soils of Australia are the poorest and shallowest of all continents, the result of millions of years of continuous weathering. There has been no widespread replenishment of soil from the Earth's interior resulting from volcanic activity. Nor has there been a cultivating effect from huge ice sheets as there was in much of North America during the Ice Age. Paradoxically, the extremely infertile soils of the sand plains of southwestern Australia have proved to be the most species diverse botanical region on the continent. Isolated from eastern Australia by the arid Nullarbor Plain, less disrupted by very dry glacial phases, and with a more consistent pattern of winter rainfall, the sand plains have spawned an extraordinary number of plant species. To date more than 10,000 have been identified, with 70 percent of them endemic to the region. No one genus or species has become dominant. The sand plains are especially rich in highly colored flowering plants such as banksias, hakeas, and grevilleas. Carnivorous plants, particularly sundews, thrive because of their ability to augment the very low levels of nitrogen in the soil with insects they catch.

A feature of this flora, and, in fact, much of the flora of Australia, is the manifestation of scleromorphy—a condition whereby the plant is often reduced in size and the leaves may be reduced to spikes or thorns. At first scleromorphy was thought to be a response to aridity and a means of reducing transpiration under increasingly dry conditions. It is now believed to be an adaptation to the extraordinary low levels of soil nutrients, particularly phosphorus and nitrogen, so characteristic of the vast majority of Australian soils.

Fire has played a critical role in the evolution of Australian flora, and Australian plants generally are particularly well adapted to respond to fire. Eucalypts, for example, grow thick, protective bark, and almost immediately after a fire send out sprouts from buds on the tree trunks or from enlarged woody roots. Other eucalypt species produce great numbers of seeds at the time of a fire that readily root in the ashes. Volatile oils in the foliage of eucalypts actually encourage fire, as does the accumulation of shed bark and leaves that builds up in the understory.

Recovery from fire can be surprisingly rapid. In February 1983 the Ash Wednesday Fire in southeastern Australia killed 70 people and destroyed hundreds of thousands of hectares of bushland and farmland. The heathlands near Anglesea, 60 miles southwest of Melbourne, were devastated, reduced to blackened stumps and white sand. Yet, in the space of three years, all but one of the more than 600 native plants that occurred in the heathlands were again flourishing. That missing plant, the rare elbow orchid, was located a few years later. Even more startling, wrinkled buttons, a plant considered extinct for more than 60 years, was rediscovered.

Like fire, the unpredictability of the weather greatly

influences agriculture in Australia and must have had a profound effect on the direction of evolution of life on the continent. In addition to anticipated seasonal fluctuations in temperature and rainfall is a meteorological phenomenon, the El Niño Southern Oscillation, or ENSO for short. Its onset is accompanied by drought on the Australian continent, particularly the eastern half. In the last 200 years Australian farmers have adjusted to this unpredictable element by conserving water and fodder, by growing plants that are drought resistant, and by stocking their properties conservatively. Long before the farmers, the Aborigines developed a nomadic system of life that allowed for the inevitable but uncertain onset and duration of drought. Like the people, Australian plants and animals have evolved so as to be able to survive this uncertain aspect of their environment.

The reproductive pattern of the female red kangaroo, for example, is closely adapted to the precarious inland habitat. Shortly before the joey in her pouch is ready to leave, a reserve dormant egg, or blastocyst, in the female begins to develop. As soon as the joey leaves the pouch, or if it dies, a newly born kangaroo makes its way to the pouch. The milk secreted from the teat to which the newly born kangaroo attaches itself is quite different from that which the joey outside the pouch continues to suckle. Soon after giving birth, the female mates. In drought conditions, however, she does not. Instead, she produces one more young from the dormant egg.

As soon as the drought breaks, the female's estrus cycle resumes, and in several months she will be associated with three stages of development: A quiescent blastocyst, a tiny kangaroo in her pouch, and a joey at her feet. In prolonged droughts, female red kangaroos, which normally begin breeding before the age of 20 months, may not breed for 3 years or more. The onset of rain, accompanied by the growth of fresh vegetation, induces an immediate response, and the animals begin breeding.

In response to climatic uncertainty an unusually high number of Australian birds have adopted a nomadic lifestyle. This applies particularly to those birds that exploit the dry inland, where the erratic nature of rainfall is accentuated and where there are frequently long periods of total drought. The budgerigar moves in large flocks to new sources of seed as soon as they become available after rain and begins breeding. Pelicans, ducks, and cormorants, normally inhabitants of the better watered coastal areas, seek out newly formed lakes and running creeks after rain.

Plants of the interior can withstand the effects of desiccation and respond quickly to the onset of rain by flowering and setting seed. These adaptations allow them to survive prolonged drought. Ephemerals, mainly of the daisy family, spring to life after heavy rain and provide a breathtaking kaleidoscope of color across the dry land. Perhaps surprisingly, succulents are not a prominent feature of the drier areas of Australia. Though able to grow in conditions of very low moisture, succulents are not adapted to the erratic rainfall pattern.

The evolution of Australian flora and fauna is a story of remarkable adaptations over 50 million years to an increasingly arid and impoverished landmass. The plants and animals of Australia developed on a continent isolated for millions of years. When explorers arrived more than 200 years ago, they found organisms new and totally different from those they knew.

The coming of Europeans has greatly increased the pressure on many of the continents' plants and animals. Forests have been cleared, grassland and heathland habitats have disappeared under crops and pastures, and salted areas have increased. Many plants and animals, such as the thylacine and the paradise parrot, have become extinct, and some 5 percent of plants are extinct, endangered, or vulnerable.

In the last 20 years there has been a gradual public awakening to the importance and the fragility of the Australian environment. With the rising land-care movement, the creation of more national parks, and government-supported programs of tree planting and habitat preservation on private land, the future looks somewhat brighter for Australia's plants and animals—flora and fauna delightfully different from those anywhere else in the world.

Following pages: *Dust veils sheep on a station near Gascoyne Junction, in Western Australia. The nearby Gascoyne River often runs dry for months at a time, but the water table below the sandy surface provides a steady source of water. When it does rain, the Gascoyne can flood spectacularly, occasionally inundating the Ten Mile Bridge near Carnarvon, some 40 miles downstream.*

Sheep await the shearer's comb in a holding pen on Bidgemia Station, in the Gascoyne River region. Shearing usually takes place around October or November, with each sheep producing several pounds of thick fleece. An experienced shearer can expect to clip more than 200 animals a day.

Harsh shadows trail a stockman in the rugged Gascoyne River country as he guides a 400-pound bale of wool onto a truck bound for market. Although Australia's economy no longer "rides the sheep's back" as it did a century ago, wool from the nation's 120 million sheep makes up 2.6 percent of the country's total exports.

Like snowdrifts in wintry twilight, massive dunes of salt await shipment in the steamy town of Port Hedland, on Australia's stark Indian Ocean coast. More than two million tons are exported from this busy port each year, a mineral wealth celebrated in the Pilbara's Fe-NaCl-NG Festival. The tongue-twisting name comes from the chemical symbols for the northwest's main exports: iron, salt, and liquid natural gas.

A surfer rides a wave off the coast of Margaret River, where beaches sport nicknames such as "Suicides," "Boneyards," and "Guillotine." Since the 1960s the area's powerful beach and reef breaks have been drawing surfers from around the world and have been the site of Australian surfing championships.

Fremantle flourished on the back of Western Australia's gold rushes in the 1890s, when so many thousands of prospectors passed through the port that authorities had to enact traffic laws governing camel trains on its streets. Nearly a century later Fremantle's Victorian architecture got a makeover when the city hosted the 1987 America's Cup Challenge.

Many hands make light work: Rowers coordinate the launch of a dragon boat on the Swan River in preparation for a Chinese New Year regatta. On weekends Perth hits its stride: Fine weather and a watery setting bring out thousands of surfers, sailors, and sunbathers. In this sports-mad, fiercely egalitarian city, more than 80 percent of river frontage is public parkland.

Following pages: *The lights of the world's loneliest city shimmer to life as the last of the sun's rays recede over the Indian Ocean. Separated by 2,000 miles of desert and mountains from Australia's eastern cities, Perth evokes a frontier feeling—a sense that the bush is never far away— that belies its modernistic skyline and air of prosperity.*

In a maneuver that would do a sheep dog proud, a shark musters salmon into shallows near the base of Western Australia's Baxter Cliffs, on the west end of the Great Australian Bight. In winter these waters, among Australia's richest fisheries, are a breeding ground for endangered southern right whales.

A leafy sea dragon flutters through cold, clear waters off the South Australia coast. The ragged membranes that give it a bizarre appearance serve as camouflage in the dense seaweed of the creature's habitat.

Lured by a slick of tuna entrails, a great white shark breaks the surface near South Australia's aptly named Dangerous Reef. Some of the largest sharks ever caught have been pulled from these waters. Here, Steven Spielberg filmed his live shark footage for the movie Jaws. Today, Australian law protects these magnificent predators.

Following pages: From a rocky perch on Dangerous Reef, black-faced cormorants scan the sea for tides and currents that signal a plentiful catch of fish. Gulls share the space and salvage any meals or leftover morsels.

Tender green shoots of coastal pigface belie this dune plant's toughness. It flourishes in the sands of Western Australia's Nuytsland Nature Reserve, a protected strip of coastline on the Great Australian Bight.

Like snowy Christmas ornaments, little corellas adorn the branches of a cypress pine. A type of parrot, these nomadic, arid-country birds live on a boom-and-bust cycle. In good years thousands flock around the outback; in times of drought their numbers swiftly decline.

Following pages: *Stately silver trunks of river red gums, largest trees in the Flinders Ranges, inspired Australian landscape artist Hans Heysen. Old-timers called these trees widow-makers because of their tendency to shed limbs unexpectedly in times of drought, sometimes killing luckless swagmen camped underneath them.*

Mouth agape, a skink hisses to ward off enemies. That sound and the reptile's defiant attitude serve as its only weapons against the hostile outback environment. Typically fat and slow-moving, these gentle lizards eat flowers, berries, and dead insects. Although they live alone, they are monogamous, seeking out the same partner each year.

Rounding one of the few bends in the line from Port Augusta, the Tea and Sugar Train rolls west across the Nullarbor Plain. Until it stopped running several years ago, the "T&S" took supplies and water to railway maintenance workers and rabbit-shooters who lived in isolated camps and siding along the line.

Following pages: *Soon after sunrise dabs of greenery stand out against red hills at Arkaroola in the North Flinders Ranges; from the air trails pinpoint an isolated research station. Human history, represented in rock paintings and carvings, dates back 30,000 years in this land of sharp-toothed peaks, carved gorges, and desert basins.*

Warped by time, the windows of the abandoned general store in Walloway, South Australia, frame plains once replete with wheat fields. The town's old schoolhouse has been restored as a weekend retreat. Faced with droughts and other hardships of life in rural Australia, many residents have fled to the cities.

Riesling grapevines planted in the 1970s edge a fence in the Clare Valley of South Australia; a house abandoned some 20 years ago now serves as a storehouse. Austrian Jesuits who arrived in 1851 established a monastery and vineyard in the area. Today, some 30 wineries exist in the valley.

Following pages: *Mirroring muted clouds, Lake Hillier spills across Middle Island in the lonely Archipelago of the Recherche; algae paints the water pink. Now a nature reserve, the scattering of a hundred granite islands off the coast of Western Australia near Esperance once lured hordes of sealers.*

Clinging to life, a tree softens a sheer granite face in the Hazards, a dramatic range of 2,000-foot-high mountains that dominates the Freycinet Peninsula, on Tasmania's eastern coast. The rugged peninsula, with its cliffs, wildflower-dotted coastal heaths, and shimmering quartzite sand beaches, was declared a park in 1916. Nearly one-third of Tasmania has been set aside as parks or reserves.

Bathed in mists, the austere profile of Cradle Mountain dominates Lake Dove, in Cradle Mountain–Lake St. Clair National Park. Dove was formed more than 20,000 years ago when glacial moraine dammed a deep valley.

Waldheim—*German for "forest home"—was built in 1912 by Austrian conservationist Gustav Weindorfer, who devoted his life to preserving the Cradle Mountain area. "Everyone should know about it and come and enjoy it," he once said—and they do. The 50-mile-long Overland Track, Australia's most popular walking trail, winds through the World Heritage site park near Weindorfer's chalet.*

Bright with blossoms, an English-style garden lends a touch of the old country to meadows and farmlands along the Derwent River Valley northwest of Hobart. Much of Australia's hops are grown near here, and the area's quaint old oasts, rows of poplars, and colonial architecture evoke England's Kent.

Following pages: *Straight lines of vines climb a curving hillside in the Tamar River Valley near George Town, on Tasmania's north coast. One of the earliest parts of Tasmania settled by Europeans, the fertile area is now the hub of Tasmania's flourishing wine industry.*

The
Heritage
Coast

CHAPTER SIX

T
he extreme southeastern coast has been the cradle of Australia's most enduring myths and icons: Convicts clanking ashore in irons at Sydney Cove in 1788, the brawling Victorian goldfields of the 1850s, colorful bushrangers such as Ned Kelly, and Banjo Paterson's legendary horseman, "the man from Snowy River." This is the home of the Sydney Opera House, the Harbour Bridge, and Australian Rules football. Melbourne and Sydney, Australia's two biggest cities, are here, and between these jealous rivals lies the carefully planned capital city of Canberra. This area, often called the Heritage Coast, is the prettiest corner of Australia in a gentle, European sense—green and well watered. In the winter snow mantles the mile-high plains of the alpine country.

The region begins near the old whaling port of Warrnambool, on Victoria's dramatic coastline west of Melbourne, and stretches almost 700 miles through rain forests and towering stands of mountain ash, the freshness of the Snowy Mountains and the Great Dividing Range, and ends in the magnificence of Sydney Harbour.

No stretch of scenery is more beautiful or dramatic than that along the Great Ocean Road, a stunning drive that winds along Victoria's cliff-lined coast for 200 miles between Warrnambool and the beachside resort town of Torquay. A public works project begun in 1918 to honor soldiers who fought in World War I, it provided work for the unemployed during the Great Depression and was completed in 1932. I cycled along it over a few days in autumn. At first a cool breeze and a few odd showers blew in off the troubled waters of Bass Strait. Then the sun broke through, bringing a sparkling seaside freshness.

The road is hilly, twisting, and narrow as it hugs the beaches and cliffs that guard this stretch of coast. Then it veers inland through dripping rain forests of the Otway Ranges before rejoining the coast near the weekend resort towns of Lorne, Anglesea, and Torquay.

The road's grandest moments are along the hauntingly beautiful rocky sentinels known as the Twelve Apostles. These weathered remnants of an ancient cliff line east of Port Campbell have become symbols of the wild grandeur, fierce gales, and pounding surf of what 19th-century mariners knew as the Shipwreck Coast.

More than a thousand ships have come to grief here. The earliest may have been a 16th-century Portuguese caravel, one of a small flotilla under the command of Cristovão de Mendonça, which some scholars believe made a secret reconnaissance of the Great Southern Land at a time when arch rival Spain was claiming much of the Pacific. That voyage, if it occurred, would be the first known exploration of Australia by Europeans. A reference to the flotilla having sailed south from Java in 1522 and a series of French maps that seem to suggest a working knowledge of Australia's southern coast are the only hints of such a journey. Mendonça's journals were believed lost in the Lisbon earthquake in 1755. In 1836, however, the hull of a strange old vessel, supposedly built of mahogany, was found in the dunes near Warrnambool. No contemporary ship was known to have been lost in these parts, and local Aborigines said the wreck had always been there. This curio remained visible in the sands until a huge storm in 1880 obliterated the site, and the origin of the "Mahogany Ship" remains one of Australia's most enduring historical mysteries.

One of the most famous shipwrecks here was the iron clipper *Loch Ard,* which ran aground off Mutton Bird Island on a foggy night in 1878. Of 54 people on board, only 2 survived—an 18-year-old sailor named Tom Pearce and 18-year-old Eva Carmichael. The tragedy moved the country, and for a time sentimentalists hoped the young survivors might marry. But the wealthier Eva Carmichael went to live with relatives in Ireland, while Pearce returned to the sea, where he was to survive two more shipwrecks in his career.

The story of the ports and bays along the southeastern coast is mostly one of whalers and sealers seeking refuge from Bass Strait's dangerous seas, fishing trawlers, historic lighthouses, and timber-fellers dragging logs to the beaches for shipment to market. But there is a genteel touch, too. Since the 1860s wealthy pastoralists in Victoria's prime sheep-grazing country around Hamilton and well-heeled gentry from Melbourne and Geelong have been coming to these breezy seaside villages for summer holidays. The advent of the automobile and the Great Ocean Road opened the area to all and sundry, and today towns such as Anglesea and Torquay are thriving resorts, thronged with visitors from Melbourne on long-weekend holidays. The booming surf cursed by last century's mariners is today's blessing, giving this stretch of coast some of Australia's finest surfing beaches. The Bells Easter Classic, held near Torquay, has been one of the top events on the world's professional surfing circuit since 1961.

Melbourne and the maritime city of Geelong got their starts on the back of a shady real estate deal. Although Matthew Flinders had sailed into Port Phillip Bay in 1802, and there had been a short-lived attempt to establish a penal colony here in 1804, the magnificent bay was unappreciated by Europeans until an entrepreneur from Van Diemen's Land named John Batman set eyes on it in 1835. He liked what he saw. "I went on shore to look at the land, which appeared beautiful, and with scarcely any timber on. On my landing I found hills of a most superior description—beyond my most sanguine expectations," he wrote. "The land was excellent and very rich—and light black soil, covered with kangaroo grass two feet high, and as thick as it could stand. Good hay could be made and in any quantity. The trees were not more than six to an acre, and those small she-oak and wattle. I never saw anything equal to the land in my life…." In what was arguably the best real estate bargain since Peter Minuit bought Manhattan for $24 worth of trade goods, Batman acquired 600,000 acres of land around Port Phillip Bay from three Aboriginal chieftains for shirts, scissors, and 50 pounds of flour.

Batman's transaction was technically illegal, despite his attending to niceties such as drawing up triplicates of the deeds of title, since the colonial office back in London did not permit independent speculation in what they regarded as crown land. Although unhappy about it, the bureaucrats let the deal stand, and two years later the town of Melbourne was laid out on a flat plain near the head of the bay, where the Yarra River flows into the sea.

The idea behind the new settlement—which was named Victoria after Britain's monarch—was that it could help service the prosperous and rapidly expanding pastoral and grazing interests in the southern part of Australia. Many of Melbourne's first settlers were gentleman farmers who built elegant homes in town from which they could vicariously manage their vast holdings in the hinterland. With money enough to have their choice of land, most of these wealthy pastoralists built on the gently rolling south bank of the Yarra River, which tends to be green and pretty. They established a trend. Over generations, the Yarra has become the defining social and economic boundary in this class-conscious city. Most of the city's prosperous middle- and upper-class suburbs—places such as South Yarra, Toorak, and Prahran—have grown on the fertile banks south of the Yarra and along the southeast flank of Port Phillip Bay. The hotter, flatter, and drier land to the north and west is generally given over to heavy industry. Fueled by huge offshore oil and gas reserves in Bass Strait and rich coal deposits in the nearby La Trobe Valley, Victoria became Australia's industrial heartland—replete with aluminum smelters, auto factories, and petrochemical plants.

Melbourne may have been founded on pastoral interests, but a string of fabulous gold discoveries around the colony in the 1850s changed everything, quickly turning the fledgling settlement into Australia's richest and biggest city, its streets lined with imposing Victorian architecture. The heady brew of gold and commerce made Melbourne Australia's banking and financial hub and home to most of the nation's largest corporations, a title it now grudgingly shares with Sydney. But there are important differences between these two money capitals. Melbourne is proudly disdainful of Sydney's nouveau riche brashness. As a former New England Yankee, I've always felt more at home in Melbourne, with its Bostonian airs. This is an intensely clubby city where imponderables like family bloodlines and old school ties—notably Geelong Grammar, the alma mater of prime ministers and business luminaries such as Rupert Murdoch—matter more than income.

Perhaps not surprisingly, given such old world shadows, Melbourne is Australia's most European-feeling city, with tree-lined streets, landscaped parks, and magnificent fin de siècle architecture. Green-and-gold trolley cars clanging along the busy city streets; fairy lights in the plane trees at the exclusive Paris End of the city, near the theaters, State House of Parliament, and the grand old Windsor Hotel; and elegant bridges across the Yarra accent this European flavor. So does Melbourne's cosmopolitan population. Vast numbers of immigrants from all over Europe, particularly Greece and Italy, came here in the years after the Second World War. The world's largest population of Greeks, after Athens, is reputedly found here, while Lygon Street is famous for its cavalcade of Italian restaurants, pastry shops, cafés and *gelateria*. Since the early 1980s the largest number of the city's immigrants have been Asians. Little Bourke and Victoria Streets, with their jumble of Chinese apothecaries, Vietnamese grocers, and dim sum restaurants, throb with the vibrancy of an Asian market. Crowded footpaths are bright with fruit stalls; butcher-shop windows are festooned with ducks, chicken feet, and pig carcasses; and the air is redolent with cooking oil and scorched spices.

Melbourne is home to some of Australia's most enduring and defining traditions, classics such as the Melbourne Cup. On the first Tuesday of every November since 1861 the entire nation has come to a halt to watch the running of this horse race at the Flemington Racecourse. The first official international test match between the English and Australian cricket teams was played in 1877 at the Melbourne Cricket Ground. And it was here that Australian Rules football was invented. Those who believe that Australian institutions must be young can

note that the Melbourne football club—formed in 1858—is older than any organized club in Europe. Melburnians have always been sports mad. Perhaps one of the reasons they could afford the time for such indulgences was that Sydney and Melbourne were the first places to adopt the eight-hour workday. By the 1890s football matches in Melbourne were drawing crowds in the tens of thousands—by far the largest in the world.

It was in the rustic villages along the Yarra Valley, on the outskirts of Melbourne, that Australia began to see itself through uniquely Australian eyes. In the late 1880s a clique of nationalistic Melbourne artists led by Tom Roberts, Arthur Streeton, Frederick McCubbin, and Charles Conder began taking their easels out to the countryside to paint the Australian landscape as it really was—hot, bright, and glary, with gnarled gum trees and sun-browned grasses. Their masterpieces owed nothing to traditionally pretty English scenes. Far from gentling their images, these Heidelberg School artists, so-called after one of the Yarra Valley villages where they frequently painted, ventured into the blinding afternoon sunlight and celebrated the heat and dust and antipodean weirdness of their native land. Charles Conder's masterpiece "A Holiday at Mentone" depicts archly Victorian holiday-makers unwinding in the purplish heat of one of Melbourne's beachside suburbs. When I look at it, I can feel the breathlessness of the afternoon and the sweat running down the gentleman's collar as he eyes the girl in a beach chair reading a book. An unashamedly Australian lifestyle was taking shape. Tom Robert's 1890 "Shearing the Rams," celebrating the working-class camaraderie in the shearing shed, is an Australian icon.

Melbourne was built on gold—some of the richest finds the world has ever known. An hour's drive north through rolling farmlands lies the town of Ballarat, in the heart of Victoria's fabled gold diggings. With a population of about 65,000, it is Australia's biggest inland city. Its grand, tree-lined streets with Italianate buildings, landscaped gardens, and classical statuary made of rare marble hint at the prodigious wealth that came out of the ground here. In the early days of 1852 armed caravans brought more than half a ton of gold each *week* from gold-rich Ballarat and Bendigo to the bank vaults of Melbourne.

The catalyst for Victoria's astonishing gold strikes was the discovery of gold near Bathurst, New South Wales, by Edward Hargraves in February 1851. Word that gold had been found triggered a stampede to the Bathurst fields, which by then had been named Orphir by Hargraves. Small wonder—one nugget alone yielded 1,272 ounces—almost 80 pounds—of gold. Irritated at losing their workers to the New South Wales goldfields, Victorian businesses put up a reward in May 1851 for the person who could find gold in *their* colony.

They didn't have long to wait. On July 5, 1851, gold was reported at Clunes, about a hundred miles northwest of Melbourne. In August gold was found near the town of Buninyong. The next month a digger stumbled onto the spectacular Ballarat goldfields. More strikes came, thick and fast, until it seemed as though all of Victoria's creek beds must be sparkling with nuggets and gold dust. At Ararat and Beaufort, Castlemaine, Creswick, and Maldon—gold seemed to be everywhere for the taking. Still more fabulous strikes were reported along the Ovens River, in the northeastern part of the colony.

Word of the bonanzas spread around the world, sparking one of the world's great gold rushes and changing the face of Victoria forever. In Melbourne shops and businesses were closed: Every able-bodied man had grabbed tools and raced for the diggings. Ships, deserted by their captains and crews, crowded the harbor. Fortune hunters flocked to Melbourne from all over the world: More than 90,000 immigrants a year landed here in the headiest days of the gold rush. Victoria's population jumped 400 percent between 1851 and 1854. By 1861 more than half a million people lived in upstart Melbourne, and it had supplanted Sydney as Australia's biggest city. Gold lured the first mass influx of Asian immigrants to Australia. Thousands of Chinese rushed to the diggings in New South Wales and Victoria. To them Bendigo was known as "Golden Mountain." When a xenophobic Victorian government tried to curtail this influx with a £10 levy on Asian migrants, the Chinese disembarked in South Australia and made their own way to the goldfields.

If Melbourne seemed like a ghost town at the height of the boom, there were riotous times at the muddy shanty settlements near the diggings. Saloons and brothels ran round-the-clock; struck-it-rich prospectors slurped champagne and showered dance-hall girls with nuggets. The most colorful entertainer was the hot-blooded Lola Montez, an exotic dancer and adventuress whose scandalous, globe-trotting career had already taken her from the court of King Ludwig I of Bavaria to the brawling California goldfields by the time she reached Victoria in 1855. Her notorious spider dance was a hot favorite with the miners, although it drew a censorious editorial in the *Ballarat Times*. In one of the town's most celebrated incidents, Montez sought out the paper's editor, Henry Seekamp, and gave him a sound thrashing with her whip—another performance that delighted the miners.

The goldfield towns reached their pinnacle of opulence and style in the 1880s. Their wide, gracious streets were lined with grandly proportioned mansions—gaudy, ornate, and nouveau riche—in rich combinations of classical, Gothic, Victorian, and Italianate styles. In Ballarat the Academy of Music, built in 1875 and embellished with a domed ceiling and opulent tiered balconies, billed acts like Victoria-born Nelly Armstrong, who would become international opera diva Dame Nelly Melba. In Castlemaine the town markets were built of stone along classical lines and topped with a statue of Ceres, the Roman goddess of the harvest. Maldon, its main street lined with deep verandas and bluestone pavements, was declared Victoria's first "notable town" by the National Trust in 1965. Most of these towns faded after the gold finally petered out in the first half of the 20th century, but they are finding their niche today as living museums, their peaceful antique streetscapes popular with tourists. Sovereign Hill, a re-creation of life in Ballarat's wild gold rush days, is one of the state's biggest drawing cards.

In 1854 Ballarat was the site of the Eureka Stockade Uprising, Australia's landmark political rebellion. The rebellion was the nearest thing the six colonies had to a civil war. And in the years since, the Eureka uprising and the rebels' flag it produced have been potent symbols of Australia's fiercely independent spirit.

The Eureka incident was brought about by a stiff fee on prospecting—30 shillings a month, or a full day's boomtown wages for a carpenter. The levy was payable whether a digger discovered gold or not, and anyone found without this license was subject to prosecution—or worse, since the revenue agents deputized to collect the fees and inspect the licenses were little more than thugs and tough ex-cons.

The Victorian government's rationale for the hated license was to discourage workers from quitting their jobs and running off to the diggings, where most were unlikely to find anything but trouble. Also, the hordes of foreigners coming into Australia would probably take away what gold they found, and officials saw in them a good opportunity for revenue raising. And, while nobody in those jackpot days quite dared to raise the point that under long-standing British law all minerals automatically belonged to the crown, a license did guarantee that the crown got at least a piece of the action.

Whatever the bureaucrats' logic, the miners' resentment is easy to understand. Digging for gold in a deep, wet mine shaft was dirty, frustrating, exhausting, and dangerous, but it seemed to be the little guy's best chance of cracking a fortune in Australia. All the best pastoral land in the new country had already been handed out by the hundreds of square miles to the wealthy or well connected. But nuggets of gold were there for the taking. There were no powerful mining interests—yet—to take up major holdings. A typical claim on the Ballarat diggings was 12 feet square—workable by a single digger of any class, creed, or color. And for once fortune actually favored the working class, since they generally had the strongest backs and the most calloused hands—traits far more valuable in a muddy mine than a private school education.

Even so, few struck it rich. Most toiled long hours for little or no reward. They lived amid squalor and disease, took daily risks in the mine shafts, and paid huge markups on everything from flour to shovels. Adding a 30-shilling-a-month license fee seemed grossly unfair. Even more infuriating was the way the law was enforced. A miner had to carry his license on his person at all times or be hauled in front of a magistrate and fined. It didn't matter if the miner was working waist-deep in water. The precious paper license had to be on his person—not back in his tent where it was dry. License checks were mad-

deningly frequent. Smirking enforcers often ordered miners to climb up out of hundred-foot shafts in order to inspect their licenses—and then returned an hour later to summon them up all over again.

By October 1854 the Ballarat diggings were smoldering with resentment. Tensions were raised even higher by the murder of a miner by a local publican who was acquitted, allegedly because he was friendly with the goldfield's corrupt administration. Over the next few weeks the hot-tempered diggers—Irish republicans, German and Italian revolutionaries, freewheeling Americans—began to talk rebellion. To this end a Canadian, Charlie Ross, raised a flag he and his wife had fashioned: the Southern Cross on a blue field. The *Ballarat Times*, edited by the same Henry Seekamp who would soon be horsewhipped by Lola Montez, came out strongly in support of the miners. He urged the end of license fees and that miners be given the right to vote and run for office.

Several hundred miners met under the Southern Cross flag on November 29th. Some burned their licenses and dared authorities to do anything about it. Bullheaded goldfields commissioner Robert Rede promptly obliged, ordering a mass license inspection. Shots were fired, the riot act was read, and some miners were arrested. The miners gathered again a few days later, this time electing an Irishman named Peter Lalor to be their leader and swearing allegiance to their new flag. The poorly armed rabble then retreated behind a hastily built stockade in a strongly Irish section of the Eureka diggings.

After a bit of sober reflection, many of the miners quietly slipped away, unwilling to take up arms against Britain. There were only 150 or so left in the stockade when 400 police and troopers launched a surprise predawn attack on the compound on the morning of December 3, 1854. The battle lasted only a few minutes, but 30 miners and 5 soldiers were killed. Peter Lalor, the leader, escaped, but his left arm had to be amputated a few days later. Most of the rest of the rebels were captured and charged with high treason.

The miners lost the battle at the Eureka Stockade, but they won the war: Melbourne juries refused to convict them. The hated license was abolished, and in its place came the miner's right, which allowed the bearer to fossick for gold for a year for a payment of one pound sterling. Miners were allowed to vote and to run for office. One of those who did was Peter Lalor, who was elected to the Victorian parliament the following year. Today, a new, 2.5-million-dollar Eureka Stockade Centre sits on the site of the encounter, and the original flag is on display in the Ballarat Fine Art Gallery.

Along with Victoria's incredible wealth came outlaws. Highwaymen—or bushrangers as Australians called them—achieved a sort of perverse folk-hero status on the outback frontier, just as they did in America's Wild West. Perhaps they were even more idealized in Australia. After all, it was founded as a penal colony. In a place ruled by the lash, any form of dissent was likely to take on heroic stature among the rank and file. Politics played a role, too. Many of the bushrangers were Irish republicans, some of them children of rebels sent to Australia in chains who saw their crimes as blows for freedom. And in the eyes of the rural poor—who were also, typically, Irish Catholics—bushrangers took on a Robin Hood aura.

Bushrangers existed from the colony's earliest days. Generally, they were escapers, or "bolters" who had fled into the bush and waylaid passersby for money, food, or supplies. Present-day Tasmania became so badly infested with bandits in the early 1800s that the governor declared martial law, fearing they might take over the island. But it wasn't until the gold rush days, when there was finally wealth worth stealing rattling along the lonely bush tracks, that the era of the bushranger reached full flower. Highwaymen like Frederick Ward (a.k.a. Captain Thunderbolt), Daniel "Mad" Morgan, and Ben Hall became cult figures. But by 1880 they had faded to footnote status beside the exploits of a 25-year-old from Victoria named Ned Kelly. Australia's most famous bushranger and national hero, he has been the subject of countless movies, ballads, songs, and biographies.

Kelly was born in 1855, the son of an Irish ex-convict and part-time cattle rustler, on a dirt-poor farm in the backwoods of Victoria's northeast. A ruggedly built brawler, Ned's first brush with the law came at the age of 15, when he was brought up on assault charges. Two years later the young hoodlum drew three years of hard labor for horse theft. He was convicted largely on the perjured evidence of a corrupt policeman who apparently wanted to be rid of a troublemaker. Kelly graduated to the big time in 1878.

The story the Kellys told was that Ned and his brother Dan came home one evening to find a police officer paying unwanted attention to their sister, and Ned gave the constable a sound thrashing. The constable claimed Ned pulled a gun and shot at him. Knowing that the policeman's story was likely to stick, Ned and Dan and two of their mates, Joe Byrne and Steve Hart, fled into the bush. An armed posse came after them, supposedly planning to administer summary justice in the bush.

But the Kelly Gang—which had been advised of police movements by sympathetic rural poor—ambushed the troopers at a place called Stringybark Creek and killed three of them. There was no turning back. For the next 19 months the Kelly Gang hid out in the wild Strathbogie Ranges of northeast Victoria, their superb horsemanship and bushcraft making a mockery of their pursuers. The myth about them grew. While the authorities saw him as a murderous ruffian who had to be stopped, Kelly considered himself an Irish political rebel and a champion of the underdog rather than an outlaw. He certainly enjoyed a strong following among the struggling farmers. One crime was especially popular: When Ned robbed the bank at Euroa in December 1878, he built a bonfire in the street and burned all the mortgage documents he could find. On another occasion, he and his gang took over the town of Jerilderie, where Ned dictated a rambling 10,000-word political manifesto that was sent to police in Melbourne.

The end came in June 1880 at the town of Glenrowan, where Kelly and his gang decided to make a stand against a trainload of troopers who were coming into the mountains to track them down. Forewarned, the troopers stopped the train a little way before the town, crept up, and surprised the gang at the Glenrowan Hotel. A furious gunfight erupted and lasted through the night. Kelly was outside the hotel when the gun battle started, and, although badly wounded in the first exchange, he might have escaped. Instead, he donned a clumsy suit of "bulletproof" armor he had made out of plowshares and charged the troopers who had his brother and mates trapped in the burning hotel. He was brought down by a shotgun blast to his legs and captured. The rest of the gang perished. When he was asked by reporters why he hadn't escaped when he had the chance, Kelly supposedly replied: "A man would be a nice sort of dingo to walk out on his mates." It was a response that epitomized the outback code of honor—of mateship, courage, and disdain for authority—that had already made Kelly a hero.

Ned Kelly's court appearance in Melbourne was Victoria's trial of the century. He was found guilty and, despite a petition for mercy bearing more than 60,000 signatures, was hanged at Melbourne Gaol on November 11, 1880.

Fed by his gallant martyrdom, Ned Kelly's aura snowballed to superhero status. In 1906 he was the subject of the world's first feature-length film, which used as a prop Kelly's original armor. *The Story of the Kelly Gang* was so sympathetic to the outlaw that nervous Victorian authorities, fearing it could provoke a popular insurrection, banned it from Kelly's old stomping ground around the Strathbogie Ranges. Kelly is still a national hero. The gallows on which he was hanged, his armor, and a death mask are among the biggest drawing cards at the Old Melbourne Gaol Museum. The town of Glenrowan, about 140 miles northeast of Melbourne on the Hume Highway, commemorates Kelly's last stand with a 20-foot statue of the outlaw in his homemade armor.

Southeast of Glenrowan, and purplish in the distance on a clear day, are the Australian Alps. I climbed the highest of Victoria's mountains, 6,514-foot Mount Bogong, on a blustery autumn day. A biting wind gusted from the south, and the valleys below were thick with clouds and rain. It was a steep and muddy climb. Dense forests dwindled to wind-stunted scrub. The last miles, across ridges of frost-cracked rock toward Mount Bogong's lonely summit, evoked Scotland rather than Australia. Stretching into the swirling mists was a chain of cairns built along the ridge top. The rocks guide hikers along the Australian Alps Walking Track, a 403-mile trek from Valhalla in the south to the outskirts of Canberra.

Australia's highest mountains are more like a series of alpine plateaus than peaks, and, although the highest range is called the Snowy Mountains, they do not have year-round snow. Still, they are unlike anything else in Australia, with their ghost gums, clear cold streams, alpine grasses and lichens, and carpet of wildflowers in the spring.

Aborigines came to these highlands every summer for thousands of years to collect bogong moths. They roasted the nutritious insects, which have a nutty flavor. But it was rich alpine grasses that drew Australian cattlemen here into the high country in the 1860s. One such cattleman was Jack Riley, said to be the inspiration for Banjo Paterson's *The Man From Snowy River,* one of the best loved poems in Australia. The ballad celebrates the legendary horsemanship, recklessness, and love of adventure of the daring cowboys of the mountains.

There was movement at the station, for the word had passed around / That the colt from old Regret had got away, / And had joined the wild bush horses—he was worth a thousand pound, / So all the cracks had gathered to the fray.

They chase the herd, hard and recklessly, mile after mile through the steep and dangerous high country until it finally races down a slope so treacherous that even these hard-riding horsemen pull up. All except one, that is. Without a second's hesitation and with a wild whoop, the man from Snowy River gallops down the slope in hot pursuit. His mates watch in awe as they see him reappear on a distant hillside, still hard on the heels of the herd, trail them, and finally turn them toward home.

And, as Paterson notes in the penultimate line of the ballad, "the Man from Snowy River is a household word today." Indeed, anybody who can recite the entire 104-line ballad from memory has a good chance of being shouted a few beers at any bush pub. Riley himself is less celebrated. He lived and worked along the Victorian side of the mountains, near the rapidly flowing headwaters of the Murray River, for half a century. He died in 1914 and is buried in an unobtrusive cemetery near the town of Corryong, about 200 miles northeast of Melbourne.

The Snowy Mountains are famous for another daring feat—not so much by rugged individualists, but by 100,000 men from some 30 nations working in concert over a period of a quarter of a century. There was no balladeer laureate to record these exploits—Paterson died eight years before the project began—but the Snowy Mountains Scheme was one of the world's greatest and most ambitious engineering projects. It came about in the heady years after the Second World War as a giant public works project to irrigate farm fields and supply hydroelectricity to the rapidly growing cities along Australia's southeast coast. Work began in 1949. Throughout the 1950s and 1960s, dams were built, tunnels were punched through mountains, power stations were constructed, and rivers were diverted. Entire towns were relocated and old sites flooded. The immensely complicated project—which cost 121 lives—wasn't completed until 1974. Perhaps the greatest marvel about the Snowy Mountains Scheme had nothing to do with groundbreaking engineering—and everything to do with the human spirit. Thousands of workers, many of them immigrants from a war-shattered Europe, and at least some of whom had fought on opposite sides of that war, came together in harmony to build a future in the sunny promise of Australia.

On the northern fringe of the Snowy Mountains, in the valley of the Molonglo River, is Canberra—Australia's carefully planned capital.

The early days of a new century, January 1, 1901, marked the birth of a new nation—Australia. After years of politicking and diplomacy, the six Australian colonies had agreed to set aside their competitive squabbling and unite under a federal government. The new nation would still be British of course—with the ruling British monarch as its head of state, the Union Jack on its flag, its laws subject to veto by Britain's parliament, and its court decisions subject to review by the privy council in London. But patriotism for queen and empire was a reliable sentiment in 1901, and few Australians were troubled by this version of nationhood.

The big issue was where to locate the new federal capital. Although arch rivals Sydney and Melbourne could both make compelling cases for earning that distinction, the new constitution cleverly stipulated that the new capital had to be in New South Wales, yet had to be at least a hundred miles from Sydney. While the new capital was being established, the seat of government would be in Melbourne.

For the next seven years a number of towns put their hats in the ring. For a while Wentworth, an outback New South Wales town at the juncture of the Murray and Darling Rivers, was a leading contender. In the end, however, after much wrangling, two royal commissions, and numerous parliamentary inquiries, a site on the grazing lands in the Yass district was chosen. It was diplomatically located between Sydney and Melbourne or, as puckish wits later observed, equally inconvenient to reach from either city. In 1911 New South Wales transferred a thousand square miles to the federal government to form the Australian Capital Territory. The port of Jervis Bay was included as an annex so that the federal government would have a seaport.

A radical young architect from Chicago named Walter Burley Griffin, who had worked with Frank Lloyd Wright, won an international competition to design the new capital. His plan called for a European-style city to be laid out on three main axes that would form what he called a parliamentary triangle, with man-made lakes and minor streets radiating outward in concentric circles. Construction began in 1913, but was interrupted by World War I and continual bickering over Griffin's controversial plans and his appointment to direct the work. Twelve years passed before Griffin's plans were formally adopted—with a few revisions that he detested. By then young Griffin and his wife, who was also an architect, had settled permanently in Australia.

Parliament House opened for business in 1927, but it was 1964 before Griffin's key feature, the lake, was completed and the city actually began to resemble his vision. The final piece of his layout was slotted into place in 1988, when a 660-million-dollar Parliament House was opened on the top of a low grassy hill at the apex of Griffin's original parliamentary triangle.

Like Canberra itself, the new Parliament House was the result of an international design competition. It was won by American architectural firm Mitchell, Giurgola, and Thorpe. To maintain the integrity of the landscape, it is built into the hilltop, and the roof is grassed over. The interior of the monumental building is magnificent. It is a showpiece of colored marble, splendid Australian timbers, marquetry depicting Australia's unique flora, and a magnificent Aboriginal mosaic titled "Meeting Place" by Michael Tjakamarra Nelson. The building houses thousands of Australian paintings, sculptures, and tapestries, as well as one of only four known original copies of the Magna Carta, the document England's King John signed in 1215 that has since become the basis of all British law.

The Australia of today is vastly different from the one that constructed the old Parliament House, now home to the National Portrait Gallery. In the decade since Queen Elizabeth II opened the new parliament building, a centenary move to launch Australia as a republic in 2001 has rapidly gained momentum. Looking to Asia for its future, self-confident, relaxed, and no longer distracted by ties to a distant Europe, Australians are questioning the need to have England's monarch as their head of state. That topic, radical only a few years ago, is today's mainstream debate. No longer do newly inducted Australian citizens swear allegiance to the queen. Her portrait is gone from most public offices, and in November 1999 Australians will go to the polls in a historic referendum to decide their nation's future.

A fast expressway links Canberra with Sydney, 190 miles to the north. To appreciate its magnificent harbor, its coves lined with yachts and mansions; the sail-like Sydney Opera House; and the Harbour Bridge, however, the best way to approach Sydney is by air or water. "The finest harbour in the world, in which a thousand sail of the line may ride with perfect security," crowed Capt. Arthur Phillip, the colony's first governor, when he delivered the first load of convicts to these shores in January 1788.

Despite its beautiful setting, Sydney was a wretched place for its first few years. It teetered on the brink of famine, and most of its population—mainly thieves, pickpockets, and prostitutes from the London slums—toiled in chains and under threat of the lash. "A more wicked, abandoned and irreligious set of people had never been brought together in any part of the world," lamented a later governor, John Hunter, in the 1790s. As Sydney grew, it became a lusty port of call for South Sea whalers. It gained notoriety for its rum trade and a mutiny in 1808 by the breathtakingly corrupt military against the colony's discipline-minded governor, Captain William Bligh of *Bounty* fame.

It was the reform-minded Governor Lachlan Macquarie, arriving in 1810, who set Sydney on the path to becoming the city it is today. After breaking the power of the military junta, which monopolized trade, he estab-lished the colony's first banks, set up its currency, and embarked on an ambitious public work's program with the aid of a convict architect named Francis Greenway. Greenway designed more than 40 buildings, including some of the colony's finest—St. James Church, the Hyde Park Barracks at Victoria Square, and the Courthouse at Windsor. Roads were laid out, bridges were built, and by the end of Macquarie's ten-year residence, Sydney was a prosperous seaport of more than a thousand buildings.

The oldest part of Sydney, where early convicts set up their first camp, is a warren of narrow streets and stone buildings nestled around the southern end of the Harbour Bridge. Known as "The Rocks," it was once the most squalid, lawless, and dangerous neighborhood in Australia. Brothels, grog shops, seamy lodging houses, and waterfront pubs crammed the narrow streets. Razor gangs, pickpockets, and thugs lurked in its rat-infested alleyways. An outbreak of bubonic plague in the early 1900s forced authorities to step in and raze many of the filthy slums. Still more were leveled in the late 1920s to make way for the Harbour Bridge. A bitter controversy erupted in the 1970s, however, over plans to demolish the rest of Sydney's oldest buildings to make way for skyscrapers. Instead, the seedy neighborhood was lovingly restored and reincarnated as Sydney's most popular tourist precinct, a picturesque enclave of Dickensian cobbled streets and old stone shop fronts that house art galleries, cafés, and fashionable boutiques.

Some of Sydney's emancipated convicts, those who were shrewd enough to see opportunity even when it came disguised in the form of banishment for life, were fast becoming wealthy citizens. By the time he died in 1838, Samuel Terry, an illiterate former convict and stonemason, owned Sydney real estate worth over £250,000 pounds. One of the wealthiest men in the nation, he was known as the Rothschild of Botany Bay. By 1836 a visiting Charles Darwin noted the staggering real estate prices, adding: "The whole population, poor and rich, are bent on acquiring wealth." That was Sydney, just hitting its stride.

Now in its third century, Sydney presents a flamboyant Manhattan-style skyline, stunningly arranged around its spectacular harbor. Two of Australia's most recognized emblems, the Opera House and the Sydney Harbour Bridge, are barely a stone's throw from Circular Quay, the bustling ferry landing where thousands of commuters arrive each morning from waterfront suburbs such as Hunters Hill, Neutral Bay, and Manly.

Sydney is an aggressive, glitzy town, the financial capital of the South Pacific and headquarters to some of Australia's biggest banks, corporations, and stockbrokerages. The city's futures market is one of the world's busiest. It is home to Australia's richest people, its tallest buildings, and its priciest real estate. Sydney's collective obsession with money, glamour, and harbor views has driven the prices of mansions in dress circle locations, such as Point Piper and Vaucluse, to eight-digit heights, while even modest homes with harbor frontage can easily fetch millions. Much as Sydneysiders love their harbor, high real estate prices have forced most of the city's 4 million residents to live well back from the water. Sydney sprawls. Although its population is modest by world standards, the metropolitan area, with 45 local government areas, covers about 900 square miles. Ascend the thousand-foot-high Sydney Tower, and you see the western suburbs spreading outward toward a line of hazy bluish peaks—the Blue Mountains.

In Sydney's early days, those mountains were a formidable barrier to inland expansion, so steep and densely forested that it took early pioneers until 1813 to find a route through them. Today, it takes about two hours by train from Sydney's gracious Central Station to the mountain resort of Katoomba. The train rolls through the sprawl of Sydney's working-class western suburbs and climbs through foothill towns.

The name "Katoomba" may be a corruption of an Aboriginal word meaning "falling water," a comment on the numerous streams that spill over the edge of the spectacular sandstone escarpment and into the thickly forested Jamison and Megalong Valleys hundreds of feet below. Katoomba and the other villages in the mountains sit on the edge of this sandstone escarpment. The view is breathtaking, and often in the early mornings the cliff-lined valleys are blanketed with thick mists. Echo Point, on the rim of the valley, is famous for its view of the Three Sisters. These stone pillars have come to symbolize the Blue Mountains. According to Aboriginal legends, they are three girls who were turned into stone by their magician father in a frantic bid to protect them as they were being attacked by a fearsome creature known as a bunyip. When the frustrated bunyip turned on the father, he transformed himself into a lyrebird. Unfortunately, in the confusion, he lost his magic wand and was unable to change anybody back.

The Blue Mountains are a part of the Great Dividing Range that runs the length of Australia's eastern seaboard. The mountains got their name from the fine mist of eucalypt oil given off by the dense forests: Billions of fine droplets diffuse the sun's rays, tinting the air, blurring the horizon, and giving the mountains their famous bluish, painted-on appearance. This bracing, eucalypt-tinged air, coupled with the mountains' refreshing climate, was thought to be therapeutic. By the 1870s the mountains were a popular retreat for wealthy invalids and Sydney's well-to-do families, who came here for their summer holidays to escape the city heat and take the air. In the 1920s the mountains were popular with adventurous honeymooners, who risked the narrow roads in their jalopies to visit Jenolan Caves, on the western flank of the mountains. Today, villages retain a quaint, turn-of-the century atmosphere. The elegant façades of grand hotels and art nouveau guest houses line the streets.

For all the gentility of the Blue Mountains, and the sometimes gentle melancholy of the Heritage Coast, Sydney is a brash, outward-looking city. Its gaze, like that of much of the continent's inhabitants, is fixed on the sunshine of Queensland, and beyond that to the bustling financial markets of Asia and the rest of the world.

Following pages: *Dawn lights morning mist rising from the surface of Lake Catani, in Victoria's Mount Buffalo National Park. Seemingly as old as the hills around it, the lake is actually man-made, created in 1908 to supply water for forest-fire fighting in the high country.*

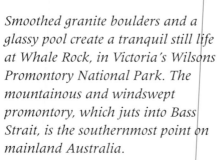

Smoothed granite boulders and a glassy pool create a tranquil still life at Whale Rock, in Victoria's Wilsons Promontory National Park. The mountainous and windswept promontory, which juts into Bass Strait, is the southernmost point on mainland Australia.

Shaped by the icy winds and blowing snow that can blast the Victorian Alps, snow gums such as these in Alpine National Park can live for nearly 500 years. A waxy film coats their leaves, buds, and flowers, protecting them from the bitter frosts of the high country. As the trees age, their smooth bark changes color from green to dusky pink, adding to their gnarled beauty.

Rushing through the densely forested flanks of the Blue Mountains in New South Wales, Jamison Creek takes a tumble at Weeping Rock on its way to much higher Wentworth Falls. The falls, one of the area's biggest attractions, was named in honor of William Wentworth, one of a trio of explorers who discovered a route through the mountains in 1813.

Cows graze steep pastures in high country near the Victorian town of Omeo, west of Alpine National Park. Since the 1860s cattlemen have driven their herds on Australia's alpine plateaus to take advantage of rich summer grasses. One of them, a hard-riding cowboy named Jack Riley, may have inspired Banjo Paterson's poem The Man from Snowy River.

by Geoffrey Sherington

A Land of Immigrants

Since its foundation as a British colony in 1788, Australia has been a land of immigrants. The colonial settlement of the Great South Land was inspired in part by the establishment of the United States of America. With the loss of the 13 American Colonies, Britain turned to "the East," seeking new opportunities for trade and a new penal settlement for convicted felons.

The convicts and many of their jailers were reluctant exiles, although many benefited from trade and some helped establish the early Australian wool industry. By the 1820s the prospect of land grants was attracting free settlers to the continent.

The European view of wealth coming from the land contrasted with the view of the indigenous population. Australian Aborigines saw land as a spiritual form to which people belonged. The philosophical gulf between the original Aboriginal peoples and the new settlers remains today, and its legacy is strong in the current discussion and debate over indigenous land rights.

The idea of wealth coming from the land lay behind the mid-19th century colonial gold rushes that transformed Australia in many ways. With the discovery of gold, the Australian continent was now seen as a land of opportunity in ways not previously imagined. Between 1851 and 1871 Australia's population quadrupled—from 437,665 people to 1.7 million. One third of those immigrants had been born in the United Kingdom.

The lure of gold also brought many immigrants from outside Britain. Prior to the strikes, few foreigners came to Australia. Only a small number of the convicts had been born outside Britain, although some had been captured in the Wars of Empire. German immigrants escaping religious persecution had settled in South Australia in the 1830s, but in the 50s and 60s large numbers of emigrants from Europe, Asia, and even North America came to dig in the goldfields of Victoria. For a period the colonial city of Melbourne became almost multilingual, with voices from many lands across the world. Not all the new settlers stayed. Like thousands of the gold seekers to California, many who rushed to Australia were sojourners out to try their luck before returning home.

Many of the gold rush generation did remain, however, particularly in the state of Victoria, which retains its legacy of gold not only in the regional centers of Bendigo and Ballarat but also in the wide, planned streets and colonial buildings of Melbourne. The country's burgeoning population would actually reinforce what had already been a feature before the discovery of gold. From the mid-19th century Australia has been one of the most urbanized societies in the world.

Despite the vast open spaces of the Australian continent, most of the new immigrants settled in the cities along the coast. Sydney had been established as a seaport, and most of the other colonial capital cities had close associations with the ocean. Most of the new arrivals settled in the capital cities such as Melbourne or Sydney. Others left the immigrant ships to try to find work along the coast, leading to the growth of the regional centers of Townsville, Rockhampton, Gladstone, and Bundaberg in Queensland. In Western Australia in the 1890s, it was the lure of gold rather than the promise of land that brought a new population to settle in the mining center of Kalgoorlie and the capital city of Perth.

From the mid-19th century to the mid-20th century, Australian governments tried to attract immigrant settlers with offers of assisted sea passages and land grants. Almost all such schemes of settling new immigrants on the land failed because much of the good land had already been claimed: Settlers of the early 19th century had taken up pastoral leases for sheep. These newcomers displaced the indigenous populations and held out against plans to divide up leases for later new arrivals. Even in the far north of Queensland many of the settlers became rural workers or sheep shearers. The shearers banded together to establish the powerful Australian Workers Union. Its formation led to conflict with the pastoralists and eventually to the formation of the Australian Labor Party as a major political force.

Trade unionism was not the only institution imported from Britain and that took a particular form in Australia. Almost all Australian political and social institutions established in the mid to late 19th century had their origins in the British Isles. Political representation came in the Westminster style, with governments formed on the basis of controlling a majority in parliament. Australian initiatives did sometimes take precedence, with the adult female franchise introduced here in 1902—before it was accepted in Britain. Universities and schools were modeled principally on British forms. Other cultural institutions, including sporting clubs and associations, often followed British examples.

By the late 19th century the dominant group in Australia consisted of English Protestants. With their religious and cultural allies, Australian Scots and Protestants from Northern Ireland, Anglo-Australians made up more than 70 percent of the population. Apart from the German settlers, the Australian-Irish Roman Catholics were the only group representing major ethnic and cultural differences. A separate Catholic school system helped maintain this difference, while the continuing English rule of Ireland left a division between Irish-Australians and those Anglo-Australians who pledged allegiance to the English monarchy.

Ethnic and religious differences were thus basic causes of sectarian animosities arising out of immigration. Forms of assimilation did emerge, however. In contrast to North America, Irish-Australians did not necessarily live alongside one another. Ethnic neighborhoods were not major features of Australian colonial cities.

Moreover, unlike other settler societies in the British Empire, such as Canada or South Africa, language was not a cultural barrier. The Irish-Australian Catholics may have had their own festivals and feast days, but they shared English as a common language with almost all other immigrants. Speaking the same language as most fellow Australians, the Irish used their own ways to express a native Australian identity. While the Roman Catholic Church became part of their cultural expression, the Irish-Australians began to predominate in the Australian Labor Party, which came to represent Australian nationalism.

During the late 19th and early 20th century Irish-Australians and other Australians of British origin united on whom they wished to exclude as future settlers. Chinese immigrants had come as gold diggers in the mid-19th century. Many then settled in goldfield towns or in cities. On grounds of race, and with efforts to protect jobs, there was a rising anti-Chinese feeling. Similarly there was opposition to the employment of Pacific Islanders in the cane fields of north Queensland. As

on the west coast of North America "great white walls" went up to remain in place for almost a century. When the six Australian colonies became a federation in 1801 the first piece of legislation enacted by the new Australian Parliament created the White Australia Policy, which effectively excluded most potential immigrants of non-Caucasian background.

For most of the first half of the 20th century the new Australian federation had a policy of continuing preference for British immigrants. Australia cooperated with Britain in "Empire Settlement," which had its heyday in the 1920s.

Various schemes brought families as well as boy and girl settlers and even child migrants. In valiant efforts to become Australian farmers ,the Empire Settlers cleared the jarrah forests of southwest Western Australia and struggled in the mallee district of northwest Victoria. Other British immigrants of these years came from British cities and settled in Australian cities or regional centers, bringing much needed industrial skills for a changing Australian economy.

Even in the era of Empire Settlement the pattern of Australian immigration was changing. Since the 19th-century seafaring sojourners from the coast of Italy and the Greek islands of the Aegean had been arriving in small numbers. The decision of the United States in 1921 to restrict its flow of immigrants led some from these Mediterranean regions to look more toward Australia. Unlike British immigrants, these settlers from southern Europe were not offered government assistance for travel or settlement.

Instead they depended on the support of kith and kin and the links of chain migration with their villages or towns. Throughout the country towns of regional Australia, Greek cafés appeared; in the cane fields of northern Queensland Italian communities formed in such centers as Ingham. Many of these European settlers went west to Kalgoorlie, leading to antiforeigner riots during the Depression of the 1930s. Only slowly did the Australian-born begin to accept these new arrivals. By the late 1930s the Australian government had at least agreed to accept a small number of Jewish refugees from Germany and central Europe.

The events of the Second World War had a major effect on Australian immigration policy. Threatened with the prospect of a Japanese invasion, Australian governments embarked on a postwar nation-building exercise to increase population. It was hoped that migrants would secure the future of the nation, contributing to economic growth and providing a bulwark against a possible threat from Australia's Asian neighbors. Despite turning more to the United States for protection and investment, Australia still looked principally to Britain to fulfill the need for new citizens. Indeed, until the 1960s, British immigrants, supported by assisted passage schemes, constituted at least half of those who arrived in Australia.

British immigration began to revive after 1945, and the war in Europe also provided a new source of potential immigrants. Coming principally from the former Baltic states of Estonia, Latvia, and Lithuania, or from Poland and parts of central Europe, people who had been displaced from their homes—or DPs (displaced persons)—formed the first major wave of postwar non-English speaking migrants to Australia. Contracted to work for two years, many were sent to camps in regional Australia. They formed the bulk of the workers who built the great Snowy Mountains Scheme, which remains the most dramatic Australian postwar nation-building project.

During the 1950s immigrants came to Australia from all across northern and southern Europe. The prewar migration chains were revived among some early settlers from the Mediterranean, but there were also new patterns of migration from mainland Greece and southern Italy. Other settlers arrived from Germany, Holland, and even from Hungary in the wake of the revolt against Soviet control in 1956. With Britain and Europe still recovering from the war, Australia once again seemed a land of opportunity, which, if not as attractive as North America, still provided prospects for secure employment and opportunities to buy a house and bring up a family.

Australian homegrown industries now depended on both skilled and unskilled migrant laborers who, in turn, became the new consumers to maintain economic growth. Almost 60 percent of the increase in the Australian work force from the 1950s to the mid-1960s was the direct result of immigration. These new settlers from Europe began to transform the pattern of Australian cities, forming enclaves if not neighborhoods in which English was not always the first language spoken in the streets and shops. Outside the cities new mineral discoveries of the 1960s brought immigrants to mining towns in Queensland and Western Australia.

By the 1970s the old Anglo-dominated Australia was slowly being transformed by these new waves of immigrants. There was still a close link between knowledge of the English language, recognition of skills, and employment opportunities. Immigrants from Britain had little problem in having their trade and other qualifications recognized. Coming from already mature industrial economies, immigrants from Germany and Holland also found that their skills were highly paid in Australia.

British immigrants as well as those from northern or even Eastern Europe were more often to be found in the affluent suburbs of Australian cities. In contrast, many of the immigrants from southern Europe, who came from rural areas in their homelands, became the foundation of the blue-collar, unskilled industrial work force. In generally low-paying jobs, southern Europeans lived in inner-city areas close to their workplaces or had to move out to the fringes of the cities. Yet many still made fortunes in such areas as construction, which was helping build the skyscrapers that were transforming Australian urban landscapes.

Home ownership among Australia's new immigrants in the 1950s and 1960s was particularly high. Having acquired a house, many of the new settlers sought to invest in the future, helping their children and grandchildren go on to further education in colleges and universities.

The earlier postwar expectation was that the new arrivals should simply assimilate to their new environment. By the 1970s, and as part of an emerging welfare state, Australian governments had adopted a new policy of multiculturalism. There was growing recognition of the need for new arrivals to retain their languages and customs from their homeland and appreciation that many needed assistance in such areas as education, health, and housing. The migrant voice was now heard in politics, although proportionately few recent arrivals became parliamentary representatives or assumed leadership in the major political parties.

The new ethnic diversity of Australia was associated with the end of the old White Australia Policy. Under the Colombo Plan of 1951 Australian governments allowed a number of young people from the British Commonwealth to come to Australia to study. With their skills in demand as the economy expanded, many stayed on.

Also admitted were refugees from China, although these were principally White Russians from Manchuria who had first left their homeland in the wake of the 1917 Russian Revolution.

As the economies of Western Europe recovered from World War II, Australia had to broaden its search for immigrants to include lands closer to the Asian region. By the late 1960s there were new arrivals from Yugoslavia and Turkey. In the 1970s refugees from armed conflict in Lebanon arrived in Australia.

A changing economic and political relationship with the Asian region helped transform the pattern of migration to Australia. By the end of the 1960s Japan had already replaced Britain as Australia's chief trading partner. Australia's involvement with the United States in the Vietnam War also left a legacy. By the late 1970s boat people fleeing from the new Communist regime in Vietnam had begun to arrive on the shores of Northern Australia. This crisis led to the first major government-sponsored migration scheme of large numbers of arrivals from an Asian country. Settled initially in camps on the fringes of Australian cities, most of these refugees from Vietnam had to take up unskilled and low-paying jobs. Some struggled to adapt to the new circumstances, but within a decade many of their children had gone on to attend university.

The arrival of Vietnamese in Australia was a watershed in the history of Australian immigration. For the past two decades ethnic origin has not been an official criterion of who shall be allowed to immigrate to Australia. While the old forms of assisted passages that existed for British migration are now gone, those arriving in Australia have come for purposes of family reunion, as refugees, or with their skills in demand. Of some 85,000 immigrants to Australia each year, less than one-fifth now arrive from Britain or Europe.

Today, settlers migrate from throughout the world, although more than half come from the Asia-Pacific region. Included among these are people from the Pacific Islands and Australia's neighbor, New Zealand, from which migrants have been coming since the 19th century. From such areas as Hong Kong and Malaysia have arrived many with highly developed skills that are in demand in the new global economy. Unlike most of those early postwar arrivals from Europe or the refugees from the wars in Lebanon or Vietnam, these new arrivals often brought in capital and invested in residential and other real estate in Australian cities.

At the end of the 20th century the multicultural nature of Australia is clearly visible, particularly in its cities. In the new shopping arcades are seen the faces of people from many nations. In the suburbs, mosques and Buddhist temples are found near older churches of the Roman Catholic and Protestant traditions and newer cathedrals of Eastern Orthodoxy.

Of the Australian capital cities, Sydney is the most cosmopolitan, receiving almost 40 percent of new immigrants. More than half the Greek postwar immigrant population of 250,000 settled in Melbourne. The city retains much of its colonial heritage but also takes pride in being the city with the largest Greek population in the world outside Greece. Brisbane, Perth, and Darwin are growing with new settlers from the Asia-Pacific region. Even Adelaide has a mixture of older and newer populations. Only Tasmania's Hobart, on an island that is losing people because of lack of economic opportunities, holds on to much of the Anglo-Australian colonial past.

For many of those who see themselves as part of the Old Australia, the new Australian multiculturalism in a global era has brought uncertainties about national identity. In effect the Old Australia was principally an assimilation of the Anglo-Australians and Irish-Australians that took almost a century to achieve.

There is now far greater diversity but also complexity in the New Australia. Less than half the people in Australia can now trace their direct descent on both their paternal and maternal lines from the British and Irish settlers of the 19th and 20th century. Those with direct descent from non-British and originally non-English speaking settlers now make up about one-quarter of the population. The fastest growing group in Australia consists of people of mixed descent—from both 19th- and 20th-century settlers, from English-speaking and non-English speaking immigrants, from Aboriginal and non-Aboriginal background.

The Australian people are now remaking themselves in a variety of ways, which may lead to new forms of identity that will transcend the old nationalities and ethnic associations they brought with them from overseas.

Cool and damp, dawn rises over the lovingly restored waterfront of Warrnambool. A boisterous haunt of sealers and whalers in its early days, Warrnambool became a major farming and wool-milling town, yet preserved enough of its historic maritime flavor to be a holiday mecca for sightseers traveling along the spectacular Shipwreck Coast.

As dawn breaks over Sydney, a solitary swimmer completes a few laps in a seawater pool in the beachside suburb of Coogee. Sydney is a city of sports fanatics. With its sheltered waters and breezy family atmosphere, Coogee, southeast of the city, has long been one of the beaches most popular with Sydneysiders.

Players break for a hearty lunch in the clubroom of Sydney's century-old Randwick Districts Cricket Club. Still wearing his leg pads, Chinese-Australian team captain Richard Chee Quee reflects the changing face of Sydney and the traditional British game of cricket. Quee has represented his state, New South Wales, in the Sheffield Shield national competition and has led cricket coaching clinics in Hong Kong.

Bluefin tuna meets the filleting knife at Claudio's Quality Seafoods in the Sydney Fish Market. Early on weekdays shopkeepers and chefs crowd the market on Blackwattle Bay, clamoring for the freshest and best fish. Sydney's thriving and cosmopolitan restaurant scene owes its existence to an influx of immigrants from Asia and the Mediterranean.

Like a giant beachside slumber
party, Wylie's Floating Film Festival
lures hundreds of arts buffs yet
reflects Sydney's relaxed and humor-
ously informal atmosphere.
Spectators at the seaside baths at
Coogee can watch from deck chairs
or paddle around on their own
rubber dinghies.

Luna Park's rictus grin, a Sydney landmark since 1935, still beckons fun lovers to the city's harborside. The amusement park closed for reno-vation in the 1980s, reopening in 1995. Sydney's lights and action attract the nation's brightest, richest, and raciest to Australia's largest and most glamorous city.

Following pages: *Sail-like roofs of the Opera House and the graceful arch of the Sydney Harbour Bridge create a romantic backdrop for a couple strolling the promenade along Farm Cove at twilight.*

New South Wales coast. Towns such as Port Macquarie, Nambucca Heads, and Coffs Harbour are nestled in estuaries or at the mouth of rivers. The temperatures here grow warmer and the landscapes more tropical. The Great Dividing Range veers closer to the coast, its rain forest-cloaked eastern flanks brooding over the coastal villages below.

About 50 miles inland is World Heritage-listed Barrington Tops National Park. A wilderness atop two massive, 5,000-foot-high plateaus, it is dramatically cut by gorges and waterfalls, flanked by rain forest, and crowned by an alpine environment of snow gums, peat bogs, and moss. Weather is notoriously fickle up here, with occasional snow flurries even in the summer months.

Another 50-odd miles farther north and considerably closer to the coast is Dorrigo National Park, with its dense subtropical rain forests. This World Heritage site sits on the edge of the Great Dividing Range. Waterfalls spill over the rim of the plateau and feed the Bellinger River, which ultimately flows into the sea at the town of Urunga. The road that switchbacks its steep way inland, up the flanks of the range, is one of the most breathtaking side trips to be had along the northern New South Wales coast.

The stretch of the Pacific Highway along the northern New South Wales coast feels more and more like a tropical version of U.S. Route 66: narrow and potholed, with roadside kitsch and cheap motels. And for many Australian families, especially during the hard economic years of the early 1990s, the Pacific Highway was very much a migrant road, taking them away from the bleak skies of the southern industrial cities toward the sunny promise of Queensland—new jobs, new lives.

Along this highway about two miles north of the tropical town of Coffs Harbour is one of Australia's classic pieces of Route 66-style roadside camp—the Big Banana. This giant concrete piece of fruit is a monument to the main local industry, and Coffs Harbour is an amiable tourist trap that offers a banana museum, tours of a banana plantation, banana milk shakes, and banana souvenirs. Australia's roadsides are uniquely rich in this sort of kitsch. Nambour, Queensland, about 180 miles farther north, is home to the Big Pineapple. In South Australia the coastal town of Kingston has Larry, the Big Lobster; the Big Merino can be gawked at in Goulburn, New

South Wales; and Glenrowan, Victoria, has a 20-foot-high mock-up of the town's favorite felon, Ned Kelly.

The lighthouse on Cape Byron marks the easternmost point on the Australian continent, and the nearby summit of 3,794-foot Mount Warning—known as "Cloud Catcher" to the Aborigines—is the first place in Australia to feel the sun's rays each morning.

To the north the architecture begins to change to the relaxed, tropical informality of the old style Queenslander home. These elegant, highly ornamental, and uniquely Australian houses are typically built of timber, have corrugated iron roofs, and are raised several feet off the ground on hardwood (termite-proof) stumps to allow cooling air to circulate under the floor. Deep, shady verandas surround them on all sides, helping to keep the inner rooms cool. They are further protected from blazing summer heat and torrential tropical rains by decorative wooden lattice and slatted blinds but are still open to any available breeze. The first time I saw one of these beautifully designed tropical masterpieces I was cycling through the little sugar-growing town of Bauple. The owners came out and, with characteristic Queensland hospitality, invited me in for dinner and to stay the night.

Queensland is Australia's holiday state and a honey pot for its sun-seeking retirees. Its status is obvious the moment you cross the border, which marks the beginning of the famed Gold Coast Stretching from Coolangatta in the south to Beenleigh in the north, this tropical coastline is blessed with 26 miles of golden, sandy beaches and more than 300 days of sunshine each year. Australians have come here for holidays for more than a century, at first in coaches from Brisbane and later by train, but it has been only since the 1950s that the strip really began to flourish. Today, it is the most glittering and shamelessly commercial beachfront in Australia, a real estate jungle of high-rises, glitzy hotels, more than 500 restaurants and nightclubs, and a cavalcade of theme parks such as Sea World, Warner Bros. Movie World, and the Disney-like Dreamworld. More than half a million people live along the Gold Coast, and there are beds for another 100,000 visitors. It is Queensland's second largest population center after Brisbane, whose extreme southern suburbs end just a few miles from where the Gold Coast begins.

Surfers Paradise, originally the name of a local hotel in the 1930s, is the heart of the Gold Coast. Here towering high-rise hotels and apartments crowd the beach so closely that by mid-afternoon most of it is in shadow. Increasingly, that hardly matters. Much of the focus is away from the surf: to the annual IndyCar Race, nightclubs, luxury resorts, casinos, golf courses, convention centers, and designer shopping arcades. The golden sand and hard blue Pacific have become a sort of luxuriant, mood-setting backdrop.

It is a matter of a surprisingly few miles from this getaway holiday ambiance to the suburban world of Brisbane. Like most of Australia's capital cities, Brisbane was founded as a penal settlement. In 1823 the governor of New South Wales, Thomas Brisbane, decided to look around for an outpost that would discourage escape. The tropical heat and remoteness of a little known coast 460 miles north seemed the very spot, and he dispatched his surveyor-general, John Oxley, to scout out a suitable site. The next year a party of convicts and soldiers was sent north aboard the brig *Amity*.

The first site, on the coast of Moreton Bay, had to be abandoned because of poor soil, and the penal camp was shifted 27 miles up the winding Brisbane River to where Brisbane stands today. As is the case with most of Australia's penal colonies, this settlement's early history was one of hardship, brutality, dysentery, scurvy, heavy leg irons, merciless floggings, and sadistic guards.

In her 1975 historical novel, *The Commandant*, Brisbane-born writer Jessica Anderson gives a description of the penal colony, as seen through the eyes of a visitor in 1830: "Then a sudden bend in the river disclosed another kind of country: on one bank pleasant wooded hills, and on the other low fields swarming with men in yellow hoeing between rows of very young wheat. They were so close that Frances could hear the unrhythmic sounds of their shifting irons and the collapsing links of chain. Overseers, carrying heavy sticks, lumbered over the unsettled soil among them, and on the perimeter of the field moved red-coated soldiers, crosses of white webbing stark against their breasts, and bayonets shining and precise against field and sky.... It was their great number perhaps or the clumsiness of their fettered movements that made them appear sub-human, like animals adapted to men's work or goblins from under the hill."

Not many civilians would have seen this prison camp, since they were not generally permitted to travel within 50 miles of the place. The penal settlement was closed in 1839, and three years later Queensland was thrown open to free settlers. They came in droves. In 1859 the new colony separated from New South Wales, and Queen Victoria named it Queensland.

Although it is close to the coast, Brisbane is very much a river-oriented city, its commercial heart enclosed in a serpentine loop and linked by seven bridges to prosperous suburbs on the opposite bank. One of the most scenic of these bridges—the Story Bridge—was the creation of John Bradfield, the designer of the Sydney Harbour Bridge. Brisbane is rich in colonial architecture: Its sumptuous Italian Renaissance National Bank Building (1885) and even grander Treasury Building (1888) are testimony to the great mining wealth that came out of Queensland after the big gold strikes in the 1870s.

For most of this century Brisbane dozed in tropical sunshine. For a few tense years during World War II it was the headquarters of Gen. Douglas MacArthur and the Allies' Pacific forces, but afterward it returned to its slumbers. As late as the 1960s the tallest building in Brisbane was the 200-foot-high clock tower on its town hall. Brisbane's fortunes changed forever in the 1980s, when it hosted two international events—the Commonwealth Games of 1982 and the World Exposition of 1988—which exposed Brisbane to the world and the world to Brisbane. Both apparently liked what they saw, and in the years since Brisbane has bloomed into a vibrant cosmopolitan city—the third largest in Australia and growing rapidly. One of the fastest growing areas is the some 90-mile-long stretch of beaches an hour's drive north of the city. It is marked on maps as the Sunshine Coast.

Caloundra, Maroochydore, and Coolum Beach— once quiet holiday towns—became some of the nation's fastest growing communities during the 1990s. In what was probably Australia's biggest internal migration since the gold rush days, thousands of families and businesses flocked north to the sunbelt. New housing estates and real estate developments are sprouting up all along this breezy stretch of coast, and the highways are busy with suburban commuters and the vans of contractors servicing the housing boom. Resort towns such as Maroochydore are now small cities with their own burgeoning satellite suburbs.

For Queenslanders, who proudly considered themselves a breed apart yet were sensitive to the way southern city folk dismissed them as provincial, the population boom was a mixed blessing. Smugness at being discovered was tempered with dismay as throngs of newcomers added their hustle and pace to the Sunshine Coast's laidback holiday atmosphere.

The hinterland is still quiet, tropical farmland: lush fields of pineapples, sugarcane, and macadamia nuts. Rising dramatically more than a thousand feet above these plantations are the Glasshouse Mountains. Capt. James Cook sighted these sheer volcanic necks from the deck of his ship as he sailed up the coast in 1770.

The exclusive resort town of Noosa Heads marks the northern end of the Sunshine Coast, where an upscale sort of holiday tranquillity still prevails. With its beautiful north-facing beach on Laguna Bay and regular, big waves, the sleepy town drew surfers from all over Australia in the 1960s and has never looked back. Now it is one of the most fashionable seaside retreats for Australia's rich and glamorous. Its streets are lined with classy restaurants, boutiques, and cafés. A zoning edict that forbids buildings to be any taller than the trees has helped maintain its small beach-town atmosphere. It helps too that its beach is protected by century-old Noosa National Park, with its thousand acres of rain forest. On the other side of the bay is the haunting coastal wilderness of Cooloola National Park, with its towering eucalypt forests, streaked cliffs, and beaches of colored sand.

World Heritage-listed Fraser Island sits a few miles off the northern end of the Cooloola Coast, accessible by ferries from Inskip Point or Hervey Bay. It is the world's largest sand island, more than 75 miles long, dotted by some 40 crystal-clear lakes and covered with lush forests, including the satinay, a rain forest tree that is found almost nowhere else. Marvelously rot resistant, the prized satinay was sought by the ship-building industry.

Logging on the island ceased in 1991. During the 1970s Fraser Island was at the center of a bitter struggle between conservationists and the sand-mining industry. The conservationists carried the day, and the island remains wild. The northern half of it forms part of Great Sandy National Park.

Because of its isolation from the mainland, Fraser Island is home to Australia's last pure strain of wild dingoes, whose bloodlines have never been mixed with dogs. In recent years their numbers have boomed, and, unable to find enough to eat, roving dingoes have become a menace. Several attacks on tourists have been reported.

Fraser Island takes its name from Eliza Fraser, the wife of the captain of the *Stirling Castle,* which was wrecked on Swain Reef, near Rockhampton, in 1836. After her husband was speared by Aborigines, Fraser and a party of survivors made their way to the island in an open boat. The Kabi Aborigines adopted her, convinced that she was the spirit of a local woman named Mamba who had somehow lost both her color and her language in the process of reincarnation. Among her new tribesmen was John Graham, an escaped convict who had been similarly adopted a year earlier. Graham, who by then spoke fluent Kabi, vouched for Fraser's Aboriginality.

A search party from Moreton Bay found the castaways two months later. Fraser's story became the basis for a series of paintings by artist Sidney Nolan and Patrick White's novel *A Fringe of Leaves.*

The rum and sugar town of Bundaberg, about 50 miles north and west of Fraser Island, is a popular port of call for round-the-world yachtsmen. A five-hour cruise from here brings the traveler to Lady Elliot Island, a tropical coral cay teeming with birds and sea turtles. Its sharp corals are littered with shipwrecks dating back to the early 19th century and stretching into the 1990s.

Small and pretty in its own right, Lady Elliot Island is also the southern starting point for one of the world's greatest—and Australia's most prized—natural wonders: the Great Barrier Reef. From here it stretches 1,250 miles along the tropical Queensland coast—a chain of brilliantly colored coral reefs, dazzling white sandbars, and green tropical islands. Although it is commonly referred to as the world's largest living thing, the Great Barrier Reef is composed of 2,500 individual reefs. Some are tiny motes only a couple of acres in size, while others extend for 38 square miles. Another 600 islands are scattered along the coast, each typically surrounded by its own fringing reefs. Altogether this World Heritage site covers 135,000 square miles.

The reefs are made of billions of tiny, brilliantly colored coral polyps, which flourish in the sunlight and warmth of these shallow, crystalline seas. Polyps form a hard exterior by excreting lime. When they die, their skeletons remain, forming limestone-like building blocks for the next generation. And so, over time, a reef gradually grows. The deepest bedrock foundations for the Great Barrier Reef go back about 18 million years, but most of the modern reef—as tourists and divers know it—was formed since the end of the last ice age about 15,000 years ago. As the world's glaciers melted, rising sea levels crept over Australia's coastal plain, flooding the lowlands and creating archipelagoes—such as the 70-odd Whitsunday Islands—from hilltops. Coral rarely grows in waters more than a hundred feet deep since, like flowers, polyps need sunlight and warmth. The rise in sea levels was slow enough for the corals to keep pace. Gradually, over centuries, the reef assumed its present shape to accommodate the changes in sea level.

There are two varieties of reefs—barrier reefs and fringing reefs. The Great Barrier Reef flanks the outer edge of the continental shelf, forming a barrier to the open ocean and creating a channel between the reef and the coast. Fringing reefs build up around the edges of islands. Most of the Great Barrier Reef islands that adorn tourist brochures are actually not on the reef at all. They are continental islands on the lee side of the barrier reef that are encrusted with fringing reefs. Lady Elliot Island is a notable exception, its cay forming a part of the reef itself, and at low tide visitors can walk its coral ledges. Heron Island, near Gladstone, and Green Island, farther north near Cairns, are also part of the Great Barrier Reef.

The language of biology and geography cannot begin to capture the sheer beauty of the reef. I had never snorkeled before visiting Cairns, in far northern Queensland, and nothing could have prepared me for the magical moment when I first put my face mask into the water. The colors that bloom in these warm waters defy description: Lurid reds and vibrant pinks mingle with yellows,

purples, and shades of white to create a dreamlike fantasia. Staghorn corals, brain corals, mushroom corals, and organ pipes—more than 400 species in all—flourish here. The spectacle becomes even more fantastic for a few moonlit nights early in summer when the corals spawn, releasing countless billions of kaleidoscopic eggs.

The labyrinthine reef complex provides food and shelter for an incredible variety of creatures: More than 1,500 species of fish, in every conceivable shape, color, and size live here. Hundreds of species of anemones, marine worms, sea stars, sea urchins, and sponges add their vibrant colors and flowing motion to the Technicolor dreamscape. The nooks and crannies in the coral shelter millions of crustaceans. More than 4,000 species of mollusks live here, including dazzlingly colorful nudibranch sea slugs and rare giant clams that can grow more than 3 feet across and weigh as much as 400 pounds. Whales, dolphins, and dugongs play in these seas. Swimming in these waters gave me the odd sensation of having dived into a particularly beautiful aquarium.

The Great Barrier Reef was declared a marine park in 1975 to protect it from—and preserve it for—the other species that was increasingly drawn to its dazzling spectacle: *Homo sapiens*. Millions of tourists flock to the reef, the islands, and far northern Queensland's tropical coast every year. Northern towns along the coastal highway project a sunny, breezy, salty image, jumping-off places for the paradises over the horizon. Rockhampton, where the Bruce Highway crosses the Tropic of Capricorn, is the gateway to Great Keppel Island, one of the coast's hard-partying island resorts. Farther up the coast Mackay and Airlie Beach are popular springboards to the Whitsunday Islands, a chain of more than 70 beautifully forested islands scattered in a passage rich in vibrant coral reefs. Townsville has nearby Magnetic Island, named by Captain James Cook because his compass behaved erratically as he sailed past in 1770. Long a popular picnic spot for tourists, Magnetic Island is rapidly becoming a rustic satellite suburb for burgeoning Townsville, with commuters taking a 20-minute catamaran ride to work.

This is Far North Queensland, or "F.N.Q." in local slang: The Deep North to the rest of Australia, who often compare it with America's Deep South. The Tropic of Capricorn serves as an antipodean Mason-Dixon line. Like Dixie, F.N.Q. has had a troubled racial history. In addition to its relations with Aborigines, in the mid-19th century Kanakas, Pacific Islanders, were imported to work the cotton and sugarcane fields in conditions of virtual slavery. Kanakas were brought over in 1863 for Robert Towns, the Sydney real estate developer who underwrote the development of Townsville. In all, more than 60,000 were brought into the country until the practice was abolished in 1904.

Nearly 200 miles north of Townsville is Cairns, with its backdrop of jungle-clad mountains, often shrouded in mist, and the blood-warm waters of Trinity Bay. This once sleepy sugar town is now a city approaching 100,000 inhabitants, and it is slowly challenging Townsville for the distinction of being Australia's biggest tropical city. Its international airport and the fact that the reef here is no more than 30 miles offshore—as opposed to more than 100 miles offshore farther south—have made Cairns the prime gateway to the Barrier Reef.

Its harbor and marinas gleam with yachts and glass-bottomed boats; the Esplanade is crowded with travel agents offering cruises or flights to the resort islands. Shop fronts are bright with diving gear. Breathtaking posters of the kaleidoscopic reefs lure visitors to booking desks for reef excursions or classes to earn diving certificates. Every evening tanned faces at the sidewalk cafés are marked with the telltale lines of divers' masks. Breathless table talk is of giant sea turtles, brilliant schools of tropical fish, and the exhilarating sense of "flying" over the edge of a coral precipice and perhaps seeing a giant tortoise slowly swimming in the rich, blue depths far below.

But Cairns looks inland as well, to the rain forests of the Atherton Tableland. One of Australia's most spectacular train journeys departs from here and switchbacks up the steep, jungled flanks of the Macalister Range and through Barron Gorge National Park to Kuranda. Every day the 130-year-old steam train, reputedly the oldest still operating in the Southern Hemisphere, makes the 21-mile journey. One of the most breathtaking sights along the way is 800-foot-high Barron Gorge waterfall, which becomes even more thunderous after heavy rains. These rain forests—with those in Tasmania—are the wettest places in Australia. Nearby Mount Bellenden Ker received a record 36.9 feet of rain in 1979.

The colonial railroad station at Kuranda, with its landscaped gardens and banks of bright tropical flowers, is possibly the most picturesque depot in Australia. Nearby is the Australian Butterfly Sanctuary. Of its more than 2,000 tropical butterflies, many are rare, including the giant, iridescent blue Ulysses.

It was this steam railway that secured Cairns fortunes. Built in 1888, it linked the city with the Hodgkinson River goldfields and with the rich volcanic farmland on the Atherton Tablelands, with its bounty of macadamia nuts, tobacco, corn, peanuts, and coffee. Given this commercial advantage, Cairns quickly overshadowed rival Port Douglas, another 45 miles up the coast. Today, residents of the tranquil and tropical village of Port Douglas might think they got the better end of the bargain after all.

The drive to Port Douglas along the Cook Highway is one of the most spectacular and unspoiled in Australia. The road hugs the shore, passes secluded white coral beaches, and dips through lush rain forests. An avenue of ornamental palms leads from the Cook Highway into the tropical village of Port Douglas. With a population of about 3,700, it is the last readily accessible town for anyone driving north. "Port," as it is known locally, was discovered in the 1980s, but despite the multimillion dollar Sheraton Mirage, three Radisson resorts, and fast catamaran service from Cairns, the village has retained its sleepy end-of-the-line atmosphere.

Almost as big a draw as the prime diving spots on the reef are the ancient rain forests of Cape Tribulation and Daintree National Park. These are some of the world's largest remaining tracts of virgin tropical rain forest and mangroves, and one of the few places in Australia where tropical rain forests meet the sea. More than 90 species of orchids grow in these dripping jungles, which are also home to such strange creatures as the cassowary, a flightless rain forest bird. The cassowary stands well over six feet tall, including a multicolored crown of bone on top of its skull. Vaguely comical looking and seemingly gawky, the bird can be extremely dangerous, easily able to kill with a kick or a butt of its plated head.

Cape Tribulation and nearby Mount Sorrow were named by Capt. James Cook, who had a number of tribulations and sorrows when he passed through here on his voyage up Australia's eastern coast in 1770. His was the first recorded passage of a European ship through the Great Barrier Reef—a venture described by later navigator Matthew Flinders as the equivalent of threading a needle. Incredibly, for the first thousand miles or so of his journey through the coral, Cook was unaware that the Great Barrier Reef existed, although he began to suspect that something was making the coastal waters unusually tranquil.

As the reef stretches northward, it veers closer to the coast, as Cook was to learn. By the time he had reached the stretch of coastline near where Cooktown is today, he found himself navigating a tortuous maze of razor-sharp coral. On the night of June 11, 1770, his ship, *Endeavour*, ran aground on the reef that now bears her name.

A frantic effort to lighten the ship by heaving ballast and six cannons overboard, as well as manning the pumps and the arrival of a high tide, allowed Cook's crew to free the ship and limp toward the coast. The drama, and the officers' sangfroid in the face of danger, mightily impressed landlubber naturalist Joseph Banks. "All this time," he noted in his journal, "the seamen worked with surprising cheerfulness and alacrity; no grumbling or growling was to be heard throughout the ship, no not even an oath (though the ship in general was as well furnished with them as most in His Majesty's service)."

The crew worked the pumps and waited for the tide. "The dreadful time now approached," reported Banks, "and the anxiety in everybody's countenance was visible enough....fear of death now stared us in the face. Hopes we had none but of being able to keep the ship afloat till we could run her ashore on some part of the main where out of her materials we might build a vessel large enough to carry us to the East Indies. At ten o'clock she floated...."

Two years earlier French explorer Louis-Antoine de Bougainville had avoided a similar grounding as he approached the north Queensland coast from the open Pacific. Hearing waves washing over the shallow coral reefs ahead—a sound he later described as "the voice of God and we obeyed it"—he veered his craft away and sailed instead into the Solomon Islands. Had he ignored the watery voice and negotiated a route through the coral maze, France might have "discovered" and claimed Australia's eastern shores.

As it was, the *Endeavour* spent the next seven weeks careened on the shore near Cooktown's present location while ships' carpenters repaired the hole in her hull. A keen naturalist, Banks enjoyed his unexpected interlude in the jungle immensely, cataloguing 186 new species of plants and writing up the first known scientific description of the kangaroo.

Before setting out again in the newly repaired *Endeavour*, the explorers climbed a coastal mountain to try to scout a passage through the maze of sharp coral. "Here we overlooked a great deal of the sea to leeward, which afforded a melancholy prospect of the difficulties we were to encounter when we came out of our present harbour," Banks wrote. "In whichever direction we turned our eyes, shoals innumerable were to be seen and no such thing as any passage to sea but through the winding channels between them, dangerous to the last degree." But, piece by piece, Cook did negotiate a passage through the reefs, sailed to the tip of Queensland's Cape York Peninsula, and there, on Possession Island, hoisted the flag and claimed the entire eastern flank of the continent on behalf of England. Binding his crew to secrecy about what they had seen along Australia's coast, he set sail through the Dutch East Indies on a course for home.

Cook's voyage, which revealed the richness, diversity, and wonders of Australia, was only the beginning. It marked the beginning of many other journeys—like mine—to explore a land that is as timeless as it is unique.

Following pages: *The moon at sunrise lends an otherworldly feel to the freshwater lakes and pearly sands along the edge of lonely Shelburne Bay, on the remote northeast flank of the Cape York Peninsula.*

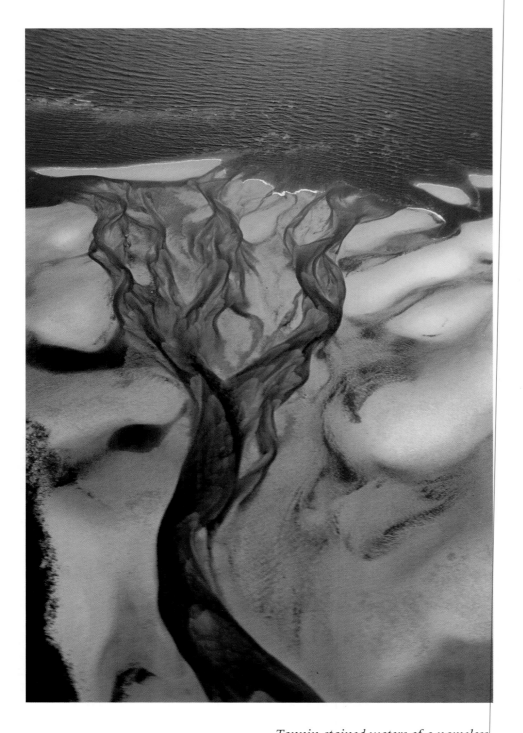

Tannin-stained waters of a nameless creek braid the sand as they meet the sea on the northeastern coast of Cape York Peninsula. Local Aborigines, who believe some of these waters harbor ancestral spirits and have traditionally hunted dugongs, turtles, and fish along these coasts, have laid claim to some areas; others have been targeted for conservation.

Heading home, Napoleon Short trails his catch, a dugong speared in the clean coastal waters south of the Lockhart River. A traditional food source for Cape York's Aborigines for eons, these gentle giants are declining in number today.

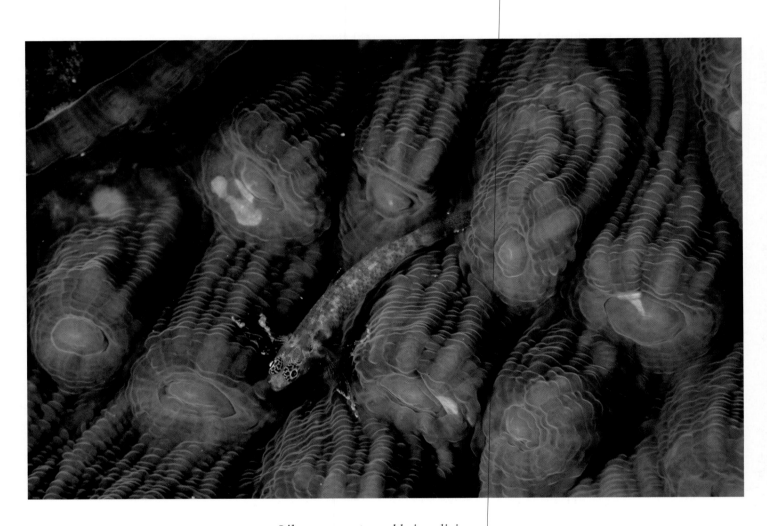

Like an errant sparkle in a living kaleidoscope, a brilliantly hued blenny-type fish darts among corals in the Great Barrier Reef. Australia's crown jewel, the vast reef complex stretches south more than 1,250 miles from the continent's northeastern tip. It hosts hundreds of species of corals, mollusks, and tropical fish.

With powerful teeth and a helmet-
like brow it has adapted for life
among corals, a Lord Howe Island
doubleheader wrasse has flipped
a sea urchin to feed on its meat
and eggs. Smaller wrasses swirl
around the encounter, waiting to
scavenge scraps left over from the
larger fish's feast.

Following pages: At low tide shallow
turquoise waters bathe Middleton
Reef, creating a swirl of color and
foam in an otherwise empty expanse
of blue Pacific about 140 miles north
of Lord Howe Island. Nearly awash
at high tide, the coral-covered
seamount has proven a deadly trap
for unwary navigators and is littered
with shipwrecks.

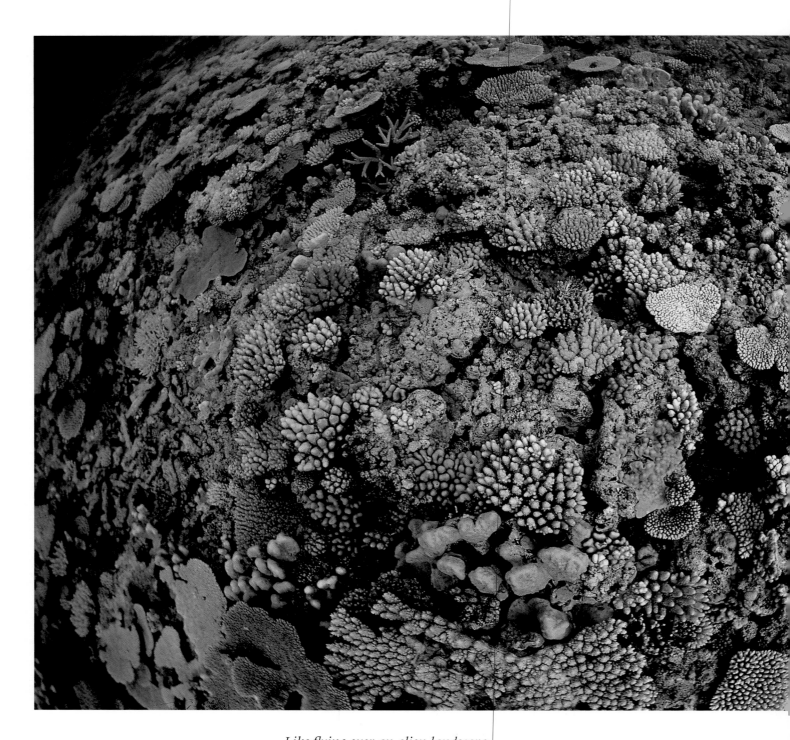

Like flying over an alien landscape: A swim through the warm shallow waters around Agincourt Reefs, off the Queensland coast near Cairns, offers a glimpse into a bommie—*a submerged chunk of hard coral. Ancient worlds in themselves, bommies can be up to 2,000 years old.*

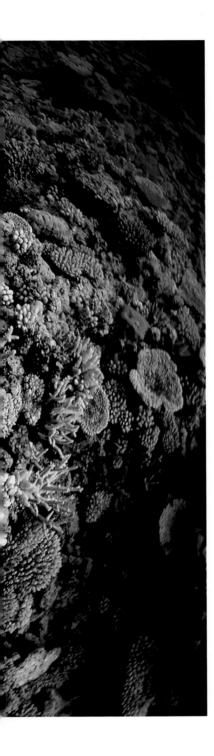

Beware of this beauty: A lionfish keeps the world at bay with a profusion of needle-sharp spines. The membrane-covered spines contain venom and can deliver an agonizing—although not lethal—wound.

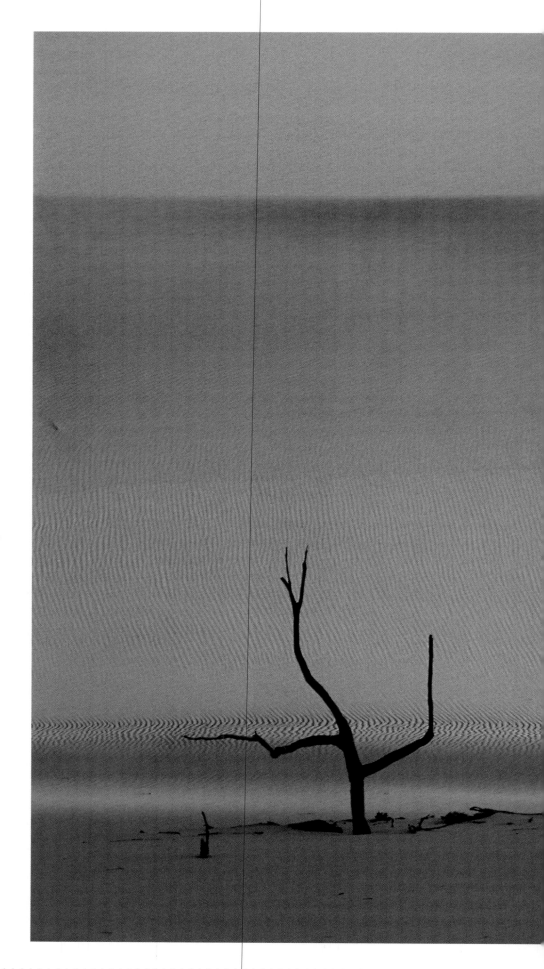

Fickle coastal breezes on Queensland's Fraser Island expose trees long buried by shifting dunes. Some 76 miles long, Fraser is the world's largest sand island and the biggest island on Australia's east coast. Although Fraser is made up entirely of sand, rain forests cloak much of the island. Specially adapted aboveground roots allow the trees to thrive on shifting sands.

Diamond-like in an immensity of mountain and rain forest, Wallaman Falls plunges a thousand feet in Queensland's Lumholtz National Park. Most spectacular during the wet season, when Stony Creek is swollen by monsoon rains, Wallaman boasts the longest drop of any waterfall in Australia.

Toiling upward, a rare green python seeks a vantage point in Cape York's Iron Range National Park, Australia's largest remaining area of lowland tropical rain forest. Found only in this remote pocket of Queensland and farther north in New Guinea, the brilliantly colored snake is a legacy of pre-Ice Age days, when a land bridge linked Australia and New Guinea.

Following pages: *Wreaths of mist rise from the hollows of Queensland's Daintree National Park. Ancient rain forests along the Daintree River are living vestiges of those that cloaked the supercontinent of Gondwana more than a hundred million years ago. Flowering plants and ferns that flourished in the Age of Reptiles still thrive here today.*

Serpentine roots of a massive fig tree deep in Iron Range National Park hint at its vast, untouched wilderness. The park shelters such oddities as the striped possum, the northern quoll (a native cat), and dozens of species of tropical butterflies. Most are found only in Cape York and New Guinea.

Mosquito net, fan, and a six-volt
battery to power it offer simple com-
forts in Brian Venable's pole-framed
house at Cape Weymouth, on the east
coast of the Cape York Peninsula.
A sense of frontier and a desire for a
self-reliant, alternative lifestyle draw
an increasing number of Australians
away from cities and into the tropical
bush of far northern Queensland.

Following pages: *Early morning
anglers greet the dawn at Byron Bay,
the first point on the Australian coast
to see the sun. The popular resort
town on the New South Wales
northern coast perches on a nearly
unbroken chain of beaches that
stretch 360 miles.*

by Harry Gordon

A Sports-Mad Country

When Australia's prime minister, John Howard, chose a couple of years ago to nominate the greatest living Australian, he did not single out a Nobel Prize winner, a World Bank president, a chief United Nations weapons envoy, an astronaut (although such people were eligible), or even a scientist, a judge, or a poet. Howard opted instead for a sportsman: a cricket player he had idolized since boyhood, Sir Donald Bradman. Bradman used to be a prolific scorer with the bat, and his deeds offered the nation comfort at times when it needed something to feel good about—during the Depression and immediately after World War II. As a captain of the Australian team, he once occupied the job that Howard considers to represent "almost the pinnacle of human achievement."

More recently, after it became publicly known that two Australian cricketers had taken money from an Indian bookmaker, Howard appeared on television, an Australian flag behind him, quite as grave-faced as when offering solace after disastrous floods and bushfires. Cricket is a game whose leisurely grace radiates a wholesome aura, and this revelation had provoked outrage and shame across the nation, even a sense of betrayal. An obviously affected Howard spoke on TV of the country's "intense feeling of disappointment" after an event he knew would "deeply disturb Australians." At this point a visitor from overseas might have been excused some degree of bewilderment. It would be truly hard to imagine any other world leader, or any other nation, reacting with such apparent agony to some shenanigans with a bookie by a couple of sportsmen. So what goes on?

The Australian prime minister is certainly an unrepentant sports buff, one who takes time on his way to visit Bill Clinton to wander around Yankee Stadium, one whose office—with its trophies, bats, balls, and photographs of champions—has the look of a small annex in a sports museum. But Howard is also a most conservative, sober politician. The truth is, his attitudes simply reflect those of his people. Australia, it needs to be understood, enjoys a serious love affair with sports. With a population of 19 million, an amiable climate, and endless beaches, the place positively pulsates with it.

To experience an Australian summer, which embraces the torpor of a long, hot Christmas holiday, is to be drenched by sports. The images of people at play are just about inescapable, which provides no problem, because most people are besotted by sports. The international cricket, tennis, and golf matches are watched on site by huge crowds—100,000 at the Melbourne Cricket Ground is fairly commonplace—and on television by millions more. On Boxing Day the entire nation watches an astonishing congestion in Sydney Harbour, as more than a hundred yachts begin the annual race to Hobart (630 nautical miles south), and a virtual confetti of small craft crowd every bay and inlet for some sort of view. The abundant beaches—and Australia is largely a coastal-dwelling nation—attract hordes: It is estimated that 8 million Australians are active swimmers. As they are buffeted in the waters around the continent, they are watched over by 27,500 unpaid surf lifesavers, 8,500 of them female. And when those on the beaches are not actually swimming, they're riding a board, sunbathing, picnicking, or playing a sandy brand of cricket that involves small children, parents, uncles, even grannies.

A 1998 survey suggests that Australians have trouble staying still. More than 2.3 million of them take to the water with some form of surfboard, 4.1 million regularly swing a golf club, and 937,000 play tennis. Twenty percent of the population (3.7 million) are active joggers, and one in three is a regular trekker through the bush. While most European nations support one code of football, Australia has settled for four—three imported, one indigenously invented—and all have large, fervent followings. The television audience for a single Australian Football League game can reach 3.5 million. For the three-minute running of a November horse race, the Melbourne Cup, the entire nation simply stops whatever it's doing, watches, and listens.

It could be argued that no other nation has defined its character and the values it cherishes more precisely through sports than Australia. These include a bluff camaraderie (known locally as mateship), a fiercely egalitarian attitude that asserts itself in a willingness to challenge authority, a tendency not just to confront adversity but to welcome it, a desire for a "fair go" (which amounts to an even break), and a laconic acceptance that you can't always win. One classic gesture and one defiant athlete have managed, in quite separate fashions, to sum up most of the distinctive elements.

The gesture involves a runner, John Landy, sacrificing an almost certain world record to go back to the aid of another athlete, Ron Clarke. Clarke had been accidentally tripped, spread-eagled on the track, then spiked as Landy leaped across his body. It happened in 1956, but the image remains etched enduringly into the Australian consciousness. Landy's action is seen not only as a sublime piece of sportsmanship, but also, romantically, as an act of mateship somehow evoking echoes of instinctive bravery among the trenches on the Somme. A sculptor, Mitch Mitchell, has immortalized it in a sculpture at the entrance to Melbourne's Olympic Park.

The defiant athlete, who happens to be the nation's most loved Olympian, is Dawn Fraser, winner of four gold medals and the first Olympic swimmer of either sex ever to win the same event three times in a row. Adversity was her beat. Discipline was her enemy. The youngest of eight children raised in a battling dockside suburb, Fraser played often as a child in a disused coal mine, suffered a variety of respiratory problems aggravated by coal dust, and was a truant and a tomboy. She left school at 14 to work in a garment factory, and by her own candid assessment was a potential delinquent. She never paid for a swimming lesson in her life, and went on to set 39 world records (27 of them individual). In 1964, during preparation for the Tokyo Olympics, she was involved in a car crash that killed her mother and injured her so badly that her neck and spine had to be encased in a steel brace for nine weeks. She won in Tokyo, but soon afterward was expelled from swimming for ten years. There had been some problems with discipline: She had marched in the opening ceremony against orders, stolen a flag, and been arrested by Japanese police.

She was 27, and the martyrdom implicit in that virtual life ban served only to enhance the legend of Fraser. Her serial conflicts with authority are seen, again romantically, to identify with those of gold miners who fought a bloody battle for their rights at the Eureka Stockade, Ballarat, in 1854.

Australia's preoccupation with sports has intrigued many visitors. A leading American sportswriter called it a land "completely surrounded by water and inundated with athletes." In the 1960s one newcomer to the country noted that being in Australia was "like living in a gymnasium. You can't look up without seeing someone practicing a sport of some kind...."

A New York writer declared in print, after a stay in Australia, that he was hard put to recall any conversation in which sports did not intrude. "If the other party is at all vulnerable," he wrote, "Australians will talk sport as if they existed for nothing else." The complaint is justified, but hardly new. As long ago as June 1892, a prominent Melbourne clergyman, the Reverend Dr. Bevan, was voicing publicly his annoyance about sport's domination of newspaper space and general conversation.

One aspect of this mania is that it doesn't play favorites. While other countries are known to go a little crazy about a single sport, such as soccer, Australia's passion pervades just about any activity that involves a contest. A measure of its intensity is provided by the knowledge that the name of Sir Howard Florey is far less well known in his homeland than those of shoals of swimmers, runners, rowers, cyclists, and tennis players. The swimmers, runners, and the rest have won gold medals, set world records, taken Wimbledon championships, enjoyed brief brushes with glory. Florey was a codeveloper of penicillin, which is credited with having saved millions of lives since 1944.

Australia's obsession with sports was seeded in the goldfields of the 1850s, where diggers indulged in bare-knuckle prize fights, footraces, and a brand of football that had a Gaelic accent but was unburdened by too many rules. It was nourished by antipodean distance, the sheer infancy of settlement, a sense of inferiority, and a yearning, in a land then split into colonies, for a feeling of oneness. Success in sport offered a kind of unifying glue, just as it helped many former convicts in that transplanted, strongly masculine society erase the awful sense of second-rateness that came with faraway memories of rejection, suppression, and poverty. By winning, it was possible to demonstrate, in the most basic way, that Australians *were* at least as good as people who lived in England and Europe. In a land with an ancient (yet seemingly brief) past and an uncertain future, sports offered rare scope for the settlers to thumb a nose at older, more established societies.

The feeling of inferiority was not just accepted: It was rubbed in. When teams from England first visited the colonies to play cricket during the summer of 1861-1862, they allowed the locals to play 22 men against their own 11. The reasoning was that the colonials might expect to be half as good as the British were. As the Australian teams improved, they fielded first 18, then 15 players, against the visiting Englishmen. When a team of 11 Australians finally beat the All-England Eleven in Melbourne in 1877 by 45 runs, the Sydney *Daily News* echoed the general mood of euphoria: "It may console them…[in London]…to note that the English race is not disintegrating in a distant land and on turf where lately the blackfellow hurled his boomerang."

The winning, and the euphoria, had in fact begun for Australia a year earlier, when a giant quarryman, a sculler called Edward Trickett, became the country's first undisputed world champion in a match race on the Thames. It took three weeks for the news to reach Australia, and when it did the *Sydney Morning Herald* reported that people didn't believe it, that it was too good to be true. When Trickett returned by ship four months later, 25,000 people waited at the wharf to greet him, along with several brass bands and all the firefighters of Sydney equipped with blazing torches. Such was the excitement that total strangers hugged in the streets.

If a moment in history might be isolated as representing the first real effusion of national pride, and the birth of a love affair with sports, "Ned" Trickett's return provided it. He was the first of a long line of heroes, and his feat offered comfort to countrymen who wanted desperately to possess an identity and share some sort of collective ego.

In the next 25 years, until the six colonies came together in federation as Australia, a variety of champions emerged. During this period, a time when those colonies were a loose bundle of neighboring territories, when there was no Australian flag, no postage stamp, and no anthem, the country made its first impact on the Olympic Games. A young accountant, Edwin Flack, who had been studying in London traveled to Athens in 1896 to take part in Baron Pierre de Coubertin's bold experiment, a revival of the ancient Greek Olympics. The experiment was hugely successful, and so was Edwin Flack.

At a time when national Olympic committees had not yet been established, Flack ran in a vest carrying the emblem of his old Melbourne school and won both the 800- and 1500-meter races. His solo expedition to Athens had another, unlikely benefit for Australian sport. Because of it, the country is able to make the rare boast that it has attended every summer Olympics of the modern era. At the 1900 Paris Games, less that a year before nationhood formally arrived, three Australians competed, and they all won gold medals.

It was in the first half of the 20th century that Australia began to develop a reputation as a nursery of sport. One pioneer was Norman Brookes, who won the Wimbledon championships in 1907 and 1914, played Davis Cup from 1905 until 1920, and began an illustrious tennis lineage. Through all this period, with odd exceptions such as opera singer Dame Nellie Melba (who happened to be the aunt of another Wimbledon champion, Gerald Patterson) Australians made little world impact in the arts.

Novelist Tom Keneally has observed that during his Sydney childhood in the 1930s, culture was something that came from another hemisphere: "What we could do was fight valiantly in wars that didn't very much concern us, produce exceptional wool and rust-free wheat, fly planes, and run, kick, swim, bat and bowl better than any race on earth." That accepted wisdom was reinforced in classrooms, where the pioneering legend of the Australian was celebrated, often in conflict with the land, the climate, the geography, and authority. It was a manly kind of legend, with little concession to the arts. Keneally detected some annoyance in the Australian cultural community toward sport, because it had been "so long seen as the appropriate response to the business of being Australian." Happily, Keneally later became one of a sizable group of Australian writers, artists, opera singers, dancers, musicians, actors, and filmmakers who made, and continue to make, a significant international impact on the arts.

The decade that still looms boldest in the landscape of Australian sporting achievement was the 1950s. A plethora of extraordinary performances occurred, one that caused the place to be recognized suddenly as a dominant force in world sports, with stature out of all proportion to its then population of some 9 million people (akin to those of Morocco and Peru). It was a period in which Melbourne hosted the 1956 Olympics (at which the home nation won a record 13 gold medals). It was a time when

Australian tennis players grabbed hold of the Davis Cup and refused to let go, simultaneously winning Wimbledon titles with what British newspapers called sad monotony.

The winning was contagious, diverse, and falsely suggestive of invincibility. Australian swimmers broke and rebroke *every* world freestyle swimming record and treated other strokes with similar contempt. John Landy and Herb Elliott ran the mile faster than anyone else, and a succession of lithe and graceful girls, from Shirley Strickland and Marjorie Jackson to Betty Cuthbert, challenged and beat the greatest Russian, Dutch, English, and German sprinters. Jack Brabham won three Formula One world driving championships, Peter Thomson took five British Open golf titles, and Russell Mockridge and Sid Patterson became world and Olympic cycling champions.

Most piquantly, rower Stuart Mackenzie echoed the deeds of the earliest practitioners of his sport by winning the Henley Diamond Sculls—the world championship of the time—not once but six times. Mackenzie, an ebullient character, was a throwback to the era when it seemed appropriate, metaphorically at least, to thumb one's nose at the British establishment, represented to him by the straw-boater gallery at Henley on Thames. Once he wore a bowler hat as he raced, and on another occasion he paddled across to a launch and splashed a spectator who had heckled him. While beating the triple Olympic champion Vyacheslav Ivanov, he took time to doff his cap and nod genially to a hooting crowd.

Inevitably the triumphs of the 1950s, particularly at the Olympics, invited theories from abroad. Factors credited for the wins included the climate, the high-protein diet, the sheer space (then around 2.3 people to the square kilometer compared to 64 in Europe), the migrant stock, even the classless nature of society. The coaching of Forbes Carlile (swimming), Percy Cerutty (athletics), and Harry Hopman (tennis) was also seen as significant.

Australia's extravagant success slowed a little in the 1960s and early 1970s, then came to a crunching halt. After John Newcombe, of Sydney, won his second consecutive Wimbledon title in 1971, the Americans, Swedes, and Germans took over. In 1976 a calamity occurred: The Australian Olympic team returned from Montreal without a single gold medal. It was the first such dismal result in 40 years, and there was much disquiet around the country. Of the many opinions to emerge from the subse-quent inquests, only two really counted. One was that, in terms of coaching and conditioning, other countries had simply caught up with Australia. The other was that, if Australia was to become a world force again, it could never rely on natural ability: It needed to spend money on overseas competition, training facilities, research, sports medicine, and the importation of coaches. Since winning the right in 1993 to host the 2000 Olympics—the second ever in the Southern Hemisphere—Australia has been spending hard and winning well, especially in swimming, rowing, shooting, and equestrian events. The women, particularly, have performed with distinction in hockey, netball, cycling, cricket, basketball, softball, basketball, and the new Olympic disciplines of the triathlon and female water polo.

Ah, those women. So long neglected, so long the victims of undisguised prejudice. For a long time Australian sport was like a stuffy club that shuddered at the thought of admitting female members. One woman, a kind of aquatic suffragette named Fanny Durack, stormed her way through a back door to raise her own fare to the Stockholm Olympics in 1912. There she won gold in swimming. Today, Durack is revered as a pioneer. Then she was a nuisance, quite as unpopular with administrators as Dawn Fraser half a century later. In the 1950s Fraser was a member of an invasion force whose superb performances caused women to be taken seriously in sport. Around her were world-beating sprinters Marjorie Jackson, Shirley Strickland, and Betty Cuthbert, closely followed by tennis players Margaret Court and Evonne Goolagong Cawley and the world squash champion Heather McKay (undefeated for 18 years).

Recent performances by athletes such as swimmers Michael Klim, Ian Thorpe, and Susie O'Neill and Aboriginal sprinter Cathy Freeman suggest that the Sydney Games, and the decade for which they will provide the overture, will echo for Australia the kind of success it enjoyed during the 1950s. Again, all kinds of theories will undoubtedly be rounded up to explain the triumphs, including those usual suspects of climate, space (a little less now, but still abundant), diet, and coaching.

In truth, though, the most significant factor will be that magnificent, enduring, and occasionally annoying obsession that had such raw beginnings on the goldfields 150 years ago.

As gray waves roll in at sunrise, a young surfer waits for her boyfriend and his mates to quit the waves off Byron Bay, on the New South Wales coast. With almost perfect beach weather year-round, the easygoing town has been a haven for surfers and backpackers since the 1960s.

A matter of perspective: Viewed through the windshield of one vehicle, a bikini-clad whale watcher uses her four-wheel drive as a crow's nest as she scans the waters off Fraser Island for humpbacks. Hunted nearly to extinction earlier this century, the whales have returned, and whale-watching has become popular with tourists and locals.

Known as the "Queen of the North,"
to the thousands of adventurers who
flocked here during the Palmer River
gold rush in the 1870s, Cooktown
boasted 65 pubs, 3 banks, and a population of more than 30,000. Today,
it is a sleepy hamlet on Queensland's
north coast and a jumping-off point
for adventurers bound for the tip of
Cape York.

Watching for his ride, a schoolboy
waits in the doorway of a shop in the
north Queensland town of Tully.
Made lush by more than 160 inches
of rain a year and rich volcanic soil,
Tully nestles in the heart of Queensland's sugar industry region. Despite
its ups and downs, sugar has largely
been sweet to the residents of Tully.
Local folklore includes a claim to
having more millionaires per capita
than any other town in Australia.

Supported by a single strand of rope, Kate Reid, artistic director of Circus Entroupe, practices violin in the northern New South Wales town of Lismore. The circus performs at nightclubs, festivals, and in Aboriginal communities around Australia. Towns in these rain forested mountains have been havens for artists and Australia's counterculture since 1974, when the Aquarius Music Festival was held in the area.

Following pages: *The pot of gold at the end of the rainbow for many Australians, Queensland's southern coast and the bustling promise of its capital city, Brisbane, lure thousands of job- and sun-seekers from around Australia. Once a distant country cousin to cosmopolitan Sydney and Melbourne, Brisbane and its suburbs now rank among the fastest growing communities in Australia.*

NOTES ON CONTRIBUTORS

Roff Smith, a New Englander who now makes his home in Seppeltsfield, South Australia, wrote three articles for the National Geographic about his 10,000-mile bicycle trip around the continent. His other contributions to the Magazine include "Nebraska: Standing Tall Again" in the November 1998 issue and "New River's Deep Soul" in June 1999.

Sam Abell has photographed for more than 20 National Geographic articles and books since 1970, including two cover stories on Australia, "Journey Into Dreamtime" and "The Uneasy Magic of Cape York Peninsula." In addition to his editorial work he maintains a career as a speaker, writer, and teacher of photography. His work is collected in the book *Stay This Moment*, which was the basis of an exhibition at the International Center of Photography in New York City.

Frank Brennan, S.J., Director of the Jesuit Social Justice Centre in Sydney, is a lawyer who is the author of several books on the subject of Aboriginal land rights.

Harry Gordon, award-winning journalist, author, and editor, writes on the Olympics for *The Australian* and is a member of Australia's Sporting Hall of Fame.

John Landy, fascinated by natural history since his childhood in Melbourne, has written the award-winning *Close to Nature* as well as *A Coastal Diary*.

Geoffrey Sherington, professor and Dean of the Faculty of Education at the University of Sydney, has written extensively on the history of immigration to Australia.

ACKNOWLEDGMENTS

The Book Division wishes to thank the many individuals, groups, and organizations mentioned or quoted in this publication for their help and guidance. In addition, we are grateful to naturalist and photographer Kerry Trapnell for his help in identifying many of the photographs and to the following: the tourist bureaus of Derby and Broome, West Australia; the Launceston Reference Library, Launceston, Tasmania; and Dr. Paul S. C. Taçon, Australian Museum, Sydney. Our thanks also to consulting editors Martha Christian and Bonnie S. Lawrence.

ADDITIONAL READING

The reader may wish to consult the National Geographic Index for related articles and books, including *Surprising Lands Down under*, by Mary Ann Harrell; *Wild Shores of Australia* by Ron Fisher; and *Voyages to Paradise* by William R. Gray. The following sources may also be of interest: Jessica Anderson, *The Commandant*; Susan Bambrick, ed., *The Cambridge Encyclopedia of Australia*; Bruce Chatwin, *The Songlines*; John J. Cove, *What the Bones Say: Tasmanian Aborigines, Science and Domination*; Robyn Davidson, *Tracks*; Tim Flannery, *The Explorers*; Lonely Planet Publications, *Australia*; Robert Hughes, *The Fatal Shore: The Epic of Australia's Founding*; Mark Twain, *Following the Equator: A Journey Around the World*.

ILLUSTRATIONS CREDITS

Photographs by National Geographic Photographer Sam Abell unless noted below.
Introduction: p. 9, Francis Birtles/Alpha; p. 12-13, David Doubilet; p. 20-21, David Doubilet. **Chapter One—The Tropical North:** p. 42-43, Mike Osborn/Kimberley Vision; p. 46-47, David Doubilet; p. 58-59, Paul Chesley. **Chapter Two—The Outback:** p. 92-93 (both), Kerry Trapnell; p. 94-95, Medford Taylor; p. 96-97, Mark Cheater; p. 100-101, Joseph J. Scherschel; p. 104-105, Rick Smolan; p. 106-107 (both), Medford Taylor; p. 108-109, David Austen; p. 110-115 (all), Medford Taylor; p. 116-117, David Austen; p. 118, Carl Purcell; p. 119-123 (all), Kerry Trapnell. **Chapter Three—The Golden West:** p. 134-139 (all), David Doubilet. **Chapter Four—The Southern Shores:** p. 180-183 (all), David Doubilet; p. 184-185 (both), Kerry Trapnell; p. 187-189 (both), Kerry Trapnell; p. 190, David Doubilet; p. 191-192 (all), Kerry Trapnell; p. 192-193, William Albert Allard, National Geographic Photographer; p. 194-197 (all), Kerry Trapnell. **Chapter Six—The Heritage Coast:** p. 234-235, Kerry Trapnell; p. 238-239, David Austen; p. 240-241, Kerry Trapnell; p. 242-243 (both), Kerry Trapnell; p. 252-255 (all), Kerry Trapnell. **Chapter Seven—A Golden Land:** p. 272-277 (all), David Doubilet; p. 292, Kerry Trapnell; p. 296-299 (all), Kerry Trapnell.

AUSTRALIA
Journey Through a Timeless Land

By Roff Smith
Photographs by Sam Abell

Published by the National Geographic Society
John M. Fahey, Jr. President and Chief Executive Officer
Gilbert M. Grosvenor Chairman of the Board
Nina D. Hoffman Senior Vice President

Prepared by the Book Division
William R. Gray Vice President and Director
Charles Kogod Assistant Director
Barbara A. Payne Editorial Director and Managing Editor
David Griffin Design Director

Staff for this book
Leah Bendavid-Val Project Editor
Toni Eugene Text Editor
Lyle Rosbotham Art Director
Sallie M. Greenwood Researcher
Carl Mehler Director of Maps
Kevin G. Craig Assistant Editor
Meredith C. Wilcox Illustrations Assistant
Natasha Klauss Research Assistant
R. Gary Colbert Production Director
Lewis R. Bassford Production Project Manager
Peggy J. Candore Assistant to the Director
Connie Binder Indexer

Manufacturing and Quality Control
George V. White Director
John T. Dunn Associate Director
Vincent P. Ryan Manager
Phil Schlosser Budget Analyst

The world's largest nonprofit scientific and educational organization, the National Geographic Society was founded in 1888 "for the increase and diffusion of geographic knowledge." Since then it has supported scientific exploration and spread information to its more than nine million members worldwide.

The National Geographic Society educates and inspires millions every day through magazines, books, television programs, videos, maps and atlases, research grants, the National Geography Bee, teacher workshops, and innovative classroom materials.

The Society is supported through membership dues and income from the sale of its educational products. Members receive NATIONAL GEOGRAPHIC magazine—the Society's official journal—discounts on Society products, and other benefits.

For more information about the National Geographic Society and its educational programs and publications, please call 1-800-NGS-LINE (647-5463), or write to the following address:

National Geographic Society
1145 17th Street N.W.
Washington, D.C. 20036-4688 U.S.A.

Visit the Society's Web site at
www.nationalgeographic.com

Library of Congress Cataloging-in-Publication Data
Smith, Roff
    Australia : journey through a timeless land / by Roff
Smith ; photographs by Sam Abell.
       p. cm.
    Includes index.
    ISBN 0-7922-7578-0 -- ISBN 0-7922-7579-9 (deluxe ed.)
    1. Australia--Description and travel. I. Abell, Sam. II. Title.

DU105.2 .S55 1999
919.404'65--dc21
                              99-023810